An American Phoenix:

A History of Storer College from Slavery to Desegregation,

COMMEMORATIVE EDITION 1865–1955

Dawne Raines Burke, Ph.D.

STORER COLLEGE BOOKS

MORGANTOWN 2015

Storer College Books / An imprint of West Virginia University Press
Copyright 2015 West Virginia University Press
All rights reserved
First edition published 2015 by West Virginia University Press
Printed in Canada

22 21 20 19 18 17 16 15   1 2 3 4 5 6 7 8 9

ISBN:

cloth   978-1-940425-77-1
pdf   978-1940425-78-8

Cataloging-in-Publication data is available at the Library of Congress

Book and jacket design by Lisa Brutto Bridges
Cover image: Harpers Ferry Naional Historic Park, Harpers Ferry, WV, USA; West Virginia Regional History Collection; West Virginia University
Editor's note: "Harper's Ferry" has been changed to "Harpers Ferry" throughout this manuscript to reflect current usage.

Table of Contents

Acknowledgments

After writing thousands of sentences on the subject of Storer College, editing scores of pages that evolved into chapters, and configuring those chapters against the image reproductions contained herein, I find this single page of acknowledgments to be most distressing, for it is impossible to acknowledge every kind word, approving gesture, and dynamic impetus that truly contributed to the book evolution of the "Phoenix Project." With so many to be thanked, it is prudent at once to offer apology to any inadvertently overlooked. I sincerely thank one and all.

I've been given but one page on which to offer my solemn yet concise acknowledgment and appreciation to representatives from the United States Department of the Interior, National Park Service assigned to the Harpers Ferry National Monument who substantially and consistently supported this effort: Nancy Hatcher, Richard Raymond, Carrie Ravenhorst, Todd Bolton, Marsha Wessel, Mike Watson, and assuredly Guinevere "Guine" Roper and Mary Robinson, who were there from the very beginning.

I commend the Storer College National Alumni Association and officers, without whose ultimate approval for this exploration I could not have proceeded any further: Mary Julia Bowles Harris, David and Juanita Cole, William "Pinch" Pinchback, Sylvia Talley, and William and Mildred Vollin. A most particular acknowledgment should be directed to my Storer College mentors, two gentlemen scholars and intellectuals, without whose fervent encouragement a serious examination of Storer College would not have been possible: Richard I. McKinney, Ph.D., a "light in the midst of darkness" who has since passed into the care of the Greatest Heavenly Light of all, and Houston G. Brooks Jr., Ph.D., a scholar whose ability to synthesize information in direct parallel with objective reasoning was and is crucial to my continued endeavors on this subject.

I acknowledge close family and friends, my mother, Wanda, and brother, Brian, The Girls, Logan Gray and D. Michael Burke, III, my children, for at least trying to understand their mother's psychological indebtedness and intellectual necessity to complete this project. To c. lynne hannah, my chair and friend, for her willingness not only to read and offer criticism on various iterations of this book draft but also—and perhaps more importantly—for her ability to understand the more convoluted, imperceptible "me" during a time of great personal and professional crisis. And thanks to all of my departmental colleagues, including Peg Swisher and Diane Plum.

Exceptional gratitude to my designer, Lisa Bridges, whose vision far exceeded my own on many occasions, and also her family, Bob, Max, and Eva Bridges, for allowing me to invade their home. My editor, Michael Slaven, Ph.D., who instantly understood that the story of

Storer should be told without delay and who also believed that my will to provide this knowledge was something to which he could unreservedly commit. I also thank Kristina Olson for her willingness to proofread the final draft manuscript in rapid fashion. Thanks to Leann Herrington, my publishing agent, whose ability to connect with the sense of urgency behind this project was most imperative.

And, finally, my most heartfelt gratitude must indeed go to Tuncer Gocmen, Ph.D., whose intellectual stimulation and professional challenge often discomforted and even infuriated me but without whose ultimate inspiration the "Phoenix Project" would have remained in a database jigsaw.

Harpers Ferry National Historical Park

I have the utmost gratitude for all those affiliated with Harpers Ferry National Historical Park. Until 1960, the government listed Harpers Ferry as "a federal monument." Its classification was then changed to that of "national historical park" into which the Storer College campus was subsumed. The school's campus then fell under the protective aegis of the United States Department of the Interior whose principal responsibility has been the histo-ecological preservation of "what is past is prologue."

If our past directs the future, according to Shakespeare's assertion, then Harpers Ferry National Historical Park protects a wellspring of human memory for this nation, its government, and its citizenry. Our government—in its purified, surest sense—should also be inclusively representative of the four philosophical cardinal pillars: "Of the people, by the people, for the people, [because of the people]" whose lives are interconnected through more than mere citizenship alone when considered in the context of one of the nation's most important sites, Harpers Ferry.

West Virginia Humanities Council

No acknowledgment is complete without including West Virginia's Humanities Council and its directing grant administrator, Amy Saunders Postalwait.

When I was appointed to the West Virginia Women's Commission by then Gov. Bob Wise, I first met Amy Saunders Postalwait at a function hosted by the commission at the West Virginia Division of Culture and History. She suggested that I appeal to the council for funding sources that might help underwrite my research topic—I was then a young, developing doctoral student.

Five documentary films later, with the support of the taxpayers and citizens of this state, I have cultivated many partnerships, cross-cultural relationships, and located community sponsors with the council's direction. I wish to extend my thanks to the council and its administrator for their guidance.

Storer College National Alumni Association

Primary sources combined with the school's physical evidence indicate that Storer alumni were routinely in contact with the school after

Acknowledgments

graduation as early as 1872, yet a formal alumni association did not evolve until 1880, when an alphabetized listing of alumni, organized according to graduation year, geographical location, and degree concentration, began to appear as an appendix in college catalogues. Institutional catalogues for the school began in 1867 with the licensure-granting approval of the state's legislature.

From Storer College's earliest beginnings, its founders wanted to inspire a sense of community. Mission school students were prepared for literate, participatory citizenship, a Jeffersonian ideal inculcated by the Board of Incorporators' Commission for the Promotion of Education in the South to ensure productive ends for not only the school and the students but also for the reconstruction of a war-torn nation.

Hence, the Storer College National Alumni Association officers and their one hundred plus constituency membership today function as advisory councils, heritage consultants, scholarship grantors, program designers, and federal partners with the United States Department of the Interior, Federal Park Division.

The community building and dedication of Storer alumni to their alma mater are a measure of the historic school's influence over the individuals they became. I was and am humbled by the association's acceptance of my application for membership into the 1880 association.

Jefferson County Black History Preservation Society

The historical preservation undertaken by the Jefferson County Black History Preservation Society in the Eastern Panhandle of West Virginia needs to be acknowledged.

Society officers have been entrusted with various and varying responsibilities for keeping track of, corresponding with, and coordinating the efforts of several organizations locally, regionally, and nationally.

In the years I have been associated with the society, it has supported designers, historians, filmmakers, producers, authors, educators, agencies, and individuals to ensure and shape our historical consciousness with regard to black history preservation in the state.

I wish to express my gratitude here to the society for its ability to bend, yet not break; yield, yet not capitulate; and for the refined demonstrations of its pride, yet with all implicit humility. I am so grateful.

Commemoration

A Tribute to Four Gentlemen Mentors: My Heavenly Quartet

Dr. Richard Ishmael McKinney (1906–2005)
Ethics and Community Building

Reclaiming the spirit of the 1906 Niagara Movement meeting held on Storer's campus, Dr. McKinney, while president at Storer College (1944–50), chartered a collegiate chapter of the National Association for the Advancement of Colored People (NAACP) and initiated an Interracial Relations Committee, both of which were institutionally necessary and overdue, yet regionally irrelevant and underappreciated. While researching and reading through an annual school administrative correspondence file in the West Virginia History and Regional Collections at West Virginia University, I noticed a phraseological tonal shift. I inquired about this in my next scheduled dissertation conversation with Dr. McKinney. I asked him about particular word choices in combination with a tonal shift—pronoun substitutions for proper nouns that I had not noticed before ("he" and "they")—that sounded somewhat prejudicially or racially imbued. Dr. McKinney thoughtfully phrased an immediate yet riveting response: "You are correct, Mrs. Burke, but I have never spoken of it." McKinney's

administration ended at Storer College in 1950, when he arranged for W. E. B. Du Bois to be the commencement speaker even though Du Bois was still under surveillance by the FBI, therefore, selecting a commencement topic far removed from the immediate gratification of those hoping to disrepute, devalue, and disfigure his mounting reputation as a member of the candidly outspoken "Black intelligentia." I posed the research-stimulated question to McKinney in 2002, just three years prior to his death. For over fifty years, McKinney maintained his peaceful sense of ethics regarding the conditions under which he was prompted to leave Storer College. Dr. McKinney was my ethics model and the progenitor for my own developing sense of community building in the enduring face of adversity.

Dr. Houston George Brooks Jr. (1927–2011)
Interconnectivity

An organic research chemist and physiologist and later Rutgers professor, Dr. Houston Brooks taught me the value of interconnective relationships through a dual lens: molecularity and bioecology. We spent several hours in conversation each week on the telephone late into the night while he coached me in the dissertation process, discussing the interconnectivity of all things on the smallest of scales. During my desolate, depressive, darkest days, Dr. Brooks, the consummate Southern gentleman, strongly urged me—although I knew he wanted to climb through the phone and shock me into a greater sense of urgency—to maintain my research objective with "progressive momentum" to connect all the pieces and look below the surface of the institutional history so that, in the final outcome, as he stressed, the institutional historiography would "be comprehensive and comprehensible" when completed. With his words etched in my mind, I set to work on the Storer history not only to ensure its structural viability but also to bring to knowledge for the first time the institution's behavioral interactivities at both the individual and organizational levels, so that the larger panoramic jigsaw pieces of its history might be routed into perspective for closer clarity with increased public exposure. Dr. Brooks often reminded me that readers should learn to know how the "institutional organism" contributed to the "concomitant march of the black man away from slavery" to become "purposeful, productive citizens." I could never repay his intellectual generosity or thank his family members enough for all the time he invested in the book's preparation. I cannot help but think that had he lived to witness this commemorative publication on the anniversary of West Virginia's statehood, he would be so proud of our accomplishment, for I could not have succeeded without his insistence to interconnect the greater story behind the institution of Storer College with the national effort to become a literate, educated citizenry, which had been the Jeffersonian ideal set into motion during the Colonial Period when men of "enlightenment" were making an effort to broaden the larger discourse and contextual influence of American government.

Mr. David Henry Cole (1924–2008)
Perseverance

I learned perseverance from David Cole, who was a star Golden Tornado football athlete at Storer College. Mr. Cole and his wife, Juanita, a Howard University graduate, were the first members of the Executive Board of Directors of the Storer College National Alumni Association (SCNAA) to invite me to their home for a day of formative discussion and archival research among Mr. Cole's personal collections. Mr. Cole was the long-standing historian for the SCNAA with a reputation for historical tenacity. He had written, filmed, and spoken publicly on the subject of his alma mater on many occasions, which I must admit was a bit intimidating for me at first. But he eventually offered to help, assist, or support in any manner by any means necessary. Building cross-cultural relationships is inescapably both personal (intrinsic) and interpersonal (extrinsic) while also time-consuming because of the concentrated energy that must be, again, both infused and invested in order to establish the trusting bridge in between. Together we learned to persevere despite the inordinate number of obstacles, difficulties, assumptions, petty jealousies, and sometimes outstanding opposition from others. I was most appreciative for having earned the trust of Mr. Cole, the institutional historian, which was something to which I was committed from the outset. We demonstrated that the impossible is indeed possible if we have steadfast objectiveness grounded in human dignity through mutual respect. As

Zimbabwe's Archbishop Desmond Tutu loudly proclaimed, "My humanity is bound up in yours, for we can only be [defined as] human [when we are] together." David Cole was the first Storer alumnus who was willing to take this leap of faith with me because of his perseverance to endure in order to promote for the people and defend for all posterity the historical contributions of Storer College to the new state and the reconstructed national union.

Mr. George Winston Hancock (1913–2004)
Empathy

Meeting George Winston Hancock was truly an answer from on high. Early in my research, I was trying to ascertain the evolutionary phases of Storer College, which led to uncovering an educational history spanning nine decades for which Hancock was the living bridge. In 1996, Mr. Hancock had been honored by then Governor Caperton with the Most Distinguished West Virginian Award, so I had heard of Mr. Hancock locally. But it was Dr. Taylor Perry at the Berkeley County School Board who arranged for my introductory meeting with Mr. Hancock. During my first meeting, I overwhelmingly sensed Mr. Hancock's empathetic responsiveness. After all, he had been the first African American promoted to the national administrative headquarters for the Young Men's Christian Association (YMCA). In that capacity, he was responsible for generating funds for massive organizational projects and new buildings. This was a burdensome responsibility, but anyone meeting George Hancock would have understood how his genuine charisma could incite people to collaborate, make persuasive appeal for consensus, and provoke synergy between and among divergent groups. Mr. Hancock was unique in having graduated three times from Storer College: the high school division (1932), the junior college (1934), and the four-year senior program (1936). After meeting Hancock, I was certain that the overlapping institutional phases were there; I just had to locate the primary source data to substantiate them. Without question, I was awestruck by Mr. Hancock's genteel demeanor and humbled by his ability to empathize not just with others but with all living beings on the planet.

EPILOGUE

For each of these black gentlemen mentors, I was their last student, a white Appalachian woman whose earliest, foundational beginnings were set against a backdrop of poverty. I am eternally indebted for their unflinching fearlessness with concomitant dedication to my education. And, in the truest spirit of Dr. Brooks, he would have proclaimed at this point, "So, now, what does color have to do with anything . . . because in the end: Everything [is] matter." I hope to be able to rejoin My Heavenly Quartet again in the great energy flow of life's next transition whatever that is, or wherever that may be.

Timeline

1650

❀ Western European ideologies correlating with intellectual skepticism and associated with the Age of Enlightenment (Reason) to the beginning of the nineteenth century are brought to North America by Rev. George Whitefield, a principal exponent of "enlightened, intellectual illumination."

1770

❀ Benjamin Randal, a skeptic among a crowd, hears George Whitefield preach, prompting Randal's religious conversion and the ultimate founding of the Free Will Baptist denomination ten years later.

❀ Benjamin Randal, founder of the New Light Separatist Baptists (Free Will Baptists), establishes the fledgling denomination's first church in New Durham, New Hampshire. On September 30, Rev. George Whitefield dies in the parsonage at the Old South Presbyterian Church in Newburyport, Massachusetts. Whitefield is regarded as one of the first preachers who routinely ministered to slaves. After his death, Phillis Wheatley writes "On the Death of the Rev. Mr. George Whitefield, 1770," a poem in his honor. The first four lines are:

> Hail, happy faint, on thine immortal throne,
> Poffeft of glory, life, and blifs unknown;
> We hear no more the music of thy tongue,
> Thy wonted auditories ceafe to throng.

1780

❀ Benjamin Randal's conversion experience and dissolution with the Calvinist ideology of predestination are described in the following passage:

> I found in Him [God] a universal love, a universal atonement, a universal call to mankind . . . Yet good men of different persuasions, have different views of the meaning of scriptures, and are naturally apt to put such constructions on them, as will best prove their favorite systems, and promote their favorite objects. The partisans of all denominations [proclaim] . . . that the scriptures are in unison with their doctrines [and go so far as to convince the general public] by any mode of allegation without any regard to their connections, put them in such order, as to make them appear to prove some darling doctrine, which they may affect to hold, under any pretext whatever, they will even dare to affirm, that all the bible goes to prove their system.

❀ Randal is ordained in New Durham, New Hampshire, on April 5.

1790

❀ The Second Great Awakening, a Protestant-revivalist movement, maintains its influence through 1820.

❀ Whitefield is the Free Will Baptist model for evangelical fervor and missionary zeal.

The denomination, during its earliest stages of evolution, will be separately and intermittently referred to as the New Lights and Separate or Separatist Baptists, Randalians, Arminian Baptists, Free Baptists, Free Will Baptists, and Freewillers.

1793

"An Act Respecting Fugitives from Justice, and Persons Escaping from the Service of Their Masters" is created through the Fugitive Slave Act, 1793, providing the legal process through which fugitive slaves were "recovered."

1796

George Washington designates a triangular 125-acre headquarter site for the United States Armory on June 15 to be a permanent arsenal in Harpers Ferry, Virginia, at the confluence of the Shenandoah and Potomac rivers.

John Storer is born on January 18 in the southeastern coastal town of Wells, Maine.

1806

William Pitt Fessenden, another Bowdoin graduate, financier, and statesman, is born in New Hampshire. He eventually moves to Portland, Maine, where he establishes his law practice.

1812

At the age of fourteen, John Storer leaves his parents and graduates from Bowdoin College.

1815

Ebenezer Knowlton, a descendant of three generations of Free Will Baptist ministers, is born on December 6. Knowlton's father, Ebenezer Sr., was also converted under the religious fervor of George Whitefield. Knowlton is a skillful legislator renowned for his ability to cultivate positive relationships; he was the primary moderator for the Free Will Baptist General Conference for several years. A member of Storer College's founding commission, Knowlton supports the school until ill health prevents his continuedparticipation in 1872.

1817

Of Scots-English ancestry, Isaac Dalton Stewart, the author of *The History of the Freewill Baptists*, born in Warner, New Hampshire, just outside Concord, on the family farm two days before Christmas. Stewart was a member of the Board of Trustees at Storer College and a member of the commission for promotion. In order to meet the conditions of Mr. Storer's will so that the Freewillers would not lose the ferry town property, I. D. Stewart "pledged his entire property in behalf of the institution" of Storer College.

Capt. John H. Hall, an inventor and gunsmith from Yarmouth, Maine, arrives in the ferry town. Hall conducts a series of experiments leading to the invention of the Hall Breechloading Flintlock Rifle and Pistol. The government quickly erects two buildings on Virginius Island in the middle of the Shenandoah River for Hall's Rifle Works.

Timeline

1819

❋ Oren Burbank Cheney, born on December 10, is from a stolidly abolitionist family. His diaries and reminiscences include entries describing frequent visits to his family home by Frederick Douglass, Harriet Livermore, and Nathaniel Peabody Rogers. Cheney, a Freewiller, is instrumental in securing buildings and funding for Storer College.

❋ Virginia legalizes illiteracy; it is illegal to educate slaves and assembling for the purpose of instruction was punishable. As John Hope Franklin Jr. later claimed, such laws were created to deter benevolent whites from teaching slaves to read.

❋ Born on December 7 in the Canadian province of Nova Scotia, George Harvey Ball believed that education was central not only to ministerial development but also to personal development. Ball accepted the position of principal at Geauga Seminary, where he taught and influenced numerous students, among whom was future president James Abram Garfield. Ball helped to establish two institutions of higher education for the denomination: Hillsdale College in Michigan and Storer College in Harpers Ferry.

1820

❋ At the age of twenty-four, John Storer marries Meribah Hobbs with whom he would have six children. Storer was working as a shipping clerk in Kennebunk for Benjamin Smith and Horace Porter when his employers suggested that he invest in a lucrative business in nearby Sanford, Maine, if Storer was willing to relocate. Together the three men initiate shipping trades with dried goods. Storer conducted business from Sanford to Portland, Maine.

❋ Maine District sheds its northern Massachusetts territory status for statehood on March 15 in conjunction with the Missouri Compromise.

1834

❋ The Free Will Baptist-Home Mission Society (FWB-HMS) is organized in Dover, New Hampshire, on July 31. The society's primary function is to invest and broker mission funds for Free Will Baptist undertakings. In its first decade, the society establishes meetinghouses, churches, and schools, and collected contributions of $5,525.78. Fifty years later, financial resources increase exponentially to enable it to allocate $85,137.60 in funds. By September 1888, the FWB-HMS had accumulated $294,564.42.

1836

❋ A native of Martinsburg, [West] Virginia, Joseph T. Hoke was the only Berkeley County representative appointed to the Commission for the Promotion of Education in the South. Hoke's family would incur much criticism for boarding mission teachers when he becomes involved with the Free Will Baptist enterprise.

1836

⊛ Nathan Cook Brackett is born in Phillips, Maine, on July 28. He will attend Phillips High School, Maine State Seminary, and Dartmouth College.

1838

⊛ By this year, Virginia made it a civil offense for free Negroes to pursue education out of state. They were banished and had to forfeit their Virginia residency if they left the state to become educated citizens.

1839

⊛ The Amistad Commission derives its name from the double-masted schooner, the Spanish slave ship *La Amistad,* which had harbored the Mende mutineers successfully defended by John Quincy Adams and Roger S. Baldwin. In 1841, the commission is organized in New York and collaborates with the Free Will Baptists.

⊛ Silas Curtis begins serving as corresponding secretary for the Free Will Baptist Home Mission Society, a position he would hold for thirty years. When the war ended, Curtis is one of the first Free Baptist emissaries to work in Virginia. He becomes a founding father of the Shenandoah Mission and eventually Storer College.

1841

⊛ Virginia is the epitome of Lincoln's "house divided against itself." Legislative documents from the period suggest that the issues of education, combined with continuing discriminatory political practices, were perhaps the greatest factors contributing to western Virginia's future separation from eastern Virginia.

⊛ On August 9, 1841, a delegation of citizens met in Kanawha County, Virginia, during the summer months to prepare "an exposition of grievances" to submit to the Virginia General Assembly. A chairperson was chosen, Judge Lewis Summers, who subsequently designated eight other members to serve with him on a committee charged to explore citizens' concerns. The Committee to Consider the Inequities of the Representation in the General Assembly of Virginia was organized by Kanawha's citizens in order "to prepare and report" the grievances of Virginia's "memorialists" to the next assembly. Based on a definitive expository grievance, the Trans-Alleghany and Valley districts unanimously adopted the Kanawha resolution, which is referred to as their "Memorial" to the General Assembly of the Commonwealth of Virginia.

1843

⊛ The Free Will Baptists recognize that denying literacy education was a method of subjugation. The "separatists" incorporate an Anti-Slavery Society. Later, in 1928, Carter G. Woodson wrote that the Baptists "had considerable communicants among the Negroes prior to the Civil War, [and] took the lead in this movement" to offer education to former slaves in the South.

Timeline

1846

⊛ The American Missionary Association, which formed after the Second Great Awakening, is established on September 3 in Albany, New York, by both whites and blacks. It is primarily a Protestant-based abolitionist group whose focus was to abolish slavery, educate illiterate blacks, promote equality through Christian ethics, and recruit teachers for "contraband" camps and mission schools. At its zenith, the association's outspoken leaders included William Lloyd Garrison, Lewis Tappan, George Whipple, Charles Grandison Finney, Simeon Smith Jocelyn, Joshua Leavitt, and Henry Ward Beecher. Three years before the American Missionary Association was founded, the Free Will Baptists had established their own Anti-Slavery Society.

1847

⊛ The Free Will Baptist women form their own organization to support and finance both foreign and domestic missions. At the triennial Free Will Baptist General Conference, held in Sutton, Vermont, the denomination's women established what was initially called the Free Baptist Female Mission Society. In 1865 it would become the Free Baptist Female Systematic Beneficence Society. The women's society, according to M. H. H. Hills, "carefully remembered" Harpers Ferry during its benevolent activities throughout its philanthropic agencies.

⊛ Constructed at a cost of $15,000, including $2,000 for the installation of a freshwater cistern, the United States Armory's superintendent's house is completed in July. It is a "two story brick dwelling with a two-story wing connected by a passageway." After the Freewillers purchase the property from the government with the government's assistance, it would be known as Anthony Memorial Hall.

1850

⊛ The Compromise of 1850—five independent yet combined congressional bills—is designed to balance slave and free states and/or territories. The Fugitive Slave Act is part of this congressional package, which legally mandated free states/territories' cooperation in the mandatory return of runaway slave chattel to their legal masters in slaveholding states/territories.

1851

⊛ Mary E. Clemmer, at twenty years of age, marries Rev. Daniel Ames, who eventually joins the Free Will Baptist effort in Harpers Ferry.

1854

⊛ Lincoln University, originally Ashmun Institute, is established in Chester County, Pennsylvania, as the first degree-granting historically black university. After graduating from Storer College in 1928, Nnamdi "Zik" Azikiwe, the first elected president of the Republic of Nigeria, attends Lincoln University, where he meets and establishes longstanding relationships with Thurgood Marshall, Langston Hughes, and Cab Calloway.

1858

❈ James Calder, who would later serve on Storer College's founding Commission for the Promotion of Education in the South, accepts the position of professor of belles lettres at Pennsylvania Female College.

1859

❈ George Tiffany Day, a member of the commission to promote for Storer College, is among several speakers addressing a large public assembly in Providence, Rhode Island, on December 2 as John Brown is executed in Charles Town, West Virginia. He prays not only for the condemned man's soul but also for the impending national strife that Day sensed would follow Brown's execution. Because of Brown's insurrection, conviction, and execution, Day grew increasingly concerned for the small denomination's education plan, which they hoped to operationalize. From the beginning, the denomination believed that one of the war's outcomes would be the freeing of slaves.

❈ Benjamin Mills, master armorer, moves into his living quarters as assigned by Armory Superintendent Clowe. The house is later occupied by Rev. Alexander Hatch Morrell with whom the house is still associated.

1860

❈ A recent graduate of Dartmouth College, Jonathan McDuffee Brewster was reared on the family farm in Wolfborough, New Hampshire. He pursued theological studies at both New Hampton and Andover, Massachusetts. Brewster had been a superintendent of public schools for North Scituate, Rhode Island. He was a member of Storer College's commission for promotion as he was a high-profile religious leader and an administrative public school officer.

❈ The census records indicate there are 463 working farms in Jefferson County, Virginia.

1861

❈ Free Will Baptist representatives are dispatched by the American Missionary Association (AMA), based in New York, to assist with the social, economic, and political milieu in Virginia. They are sent to Fortress Monroe when Gen. Benjamin "Peg Leg" Butler is confronted with the "Fortress Monroe Incident"—three runaway slaves, whom Butler calls "contraband of war" and not slave fugitives or runaway properties.

❈ On May 24, 1861, General Butler refuses to return three slaves—Shepherd Mallory, Frank Baker, and James Townsend—to Confederate Col. Charles K. Mallory, claiming he is "under no constitutional obligations" to acknowledge Mallory, citing four legal reasons: (1) the preceding week, on May 17, Virginia seceded from the Union; (2) declared state's sovereignty; (3) abrogated the United States Constitution; and (4) formed a coalition with other Confederate states, all of which constitute enemy collusion. Butler viewed himself in federal occupation of a "foreign body" under direct orders from the Union's commander-in-chief, the United States president.

⊛ In 1861, Ames had been working as a storekeeper for the federal government in Harpers Ferry when the town was taken under Confederate authority.

⊛ Following the Wheeling Convention, fifty northwestern Virginia counties secede from the State of Virginia with the onset of the Civil War in America.

1862

⊛ On the evening of October 2, President Abraham Lincoln boards his private train car from Washington bound for Harpers Ferry under heavy guard on his way to visit Maj. Gen. George B. McClellan. McClellan's army was encamped across the Potomac River in nearby Sharpsburg, Maryland, recovering from the Battle of Antietam [Sharpsburg], which had occurred two weeks earlier on September 17. Lincoln relieves McClellan of his command for failing to pursue the Confederates after the battle. Lincoln returns to Harpers Ferry to stay in Anthony Memorial Hall with the Armory superintendent.

⊛ In 1857, Professor Jonathan Baldwin Turner, who taught at Illinois College, called for the establishment of "agricultural schools" throughout the country. A "land granting statute" was proposed by Rep. Justin Smith Morrill from Vermont. Although the document was passed by the United States Congress in 1859, President James Buchanan vetoed it. The [First] Morrill Act, which would provide a land-grant college for each state, was resubmitted for ratification.

⊛ Gen. Benjamin "Peg Leg" Butler is reassigned to Louisiana for a short period during which he musters two regiments of freedmen, known as Butler's Corps d'Afrique, in which freedmen act on their own behalf, even as commanding officers. Slavery is abolished in Washington, the nation's capital, in April. "[T]he unfinished and desecrated capital" had been blemished by the presence of "slavermongers" and "slave drivers" prodding chained slaves marching through the streets. Northerners visiting the capital were "shocked grievously" by the sight. Until 1850, Washington had served as the collection site or slave depot for slaves waiting to be "sold down the river." The slaves were temporarily held in the capital until they boarded trains and ships, destined for sale in slave states.

1863

⊛ Although the preliminary version of the Proclamation was issued in September of the preceding year, the final draft of the Emancipation Proclamation is signed by President Abraham Lincoln on January 1.

⊛ West Virginia, a keystone border state between the North and the South, secedes from Virginia and achieves statehood on June 20.

⊛ The [Freewill] Baptist Freedmen's Association begins working exclusively in North Carolina and Virginia.

On August 1, General Meade orders Gen. Henry Hayes Lockwood's garrison to defend the Potomac River from Harpers Ferry to Williamsport, Maryland, "in view of the probability of the return of Lee or a part of his army into Maryland."

1864

Nathan Cook Brackett graduates from Dartmouth College, serves as an army chaplain and delegate to the United States Christian Commission, and is attached to Maj. Gen. Philip Henry Sheridan, Army of the Shenandoah. Sheridan was in Harpers Ferry on August 7, 1864, and throughout the region to prevent the largely agricultural valley from becoming the "breadbasket of the confederacy." Sheridan situates his command center at Lockwood House.

Brackett subsequently receives correspondence from Silas Curtis, secretary for the Free Will Baptist-Home Mission Society, asking him to consider Harpers Ferry as the site for the "Southern enterprise" because "it is of historical value."

After attending Rock River Seminary, Oberlin College, and Hillsdale College, John T. Hoke graduates from Michigan University with a degree in legal studies. Hoke returns to his native Martinsburg, where he is admitted to the Berkeley County bar in the Union's newly formed thirty-fifth state of West Virginia. Storer College owes it ultimate charter, in the wake of lingering confederation sympathies, as a school "without distinction" to senator and statesman Joseph T. Hoke. The senator resigned his position from the commission for the promotion so that he could "cast the decisive vote, for the success of the measure turned upon his foresight and the Act passed by one [stet] majority" in the legislature in 1868.

Brackett helps a young woman, Julia Mann, with her school for war indigents and slave refugees through the harsh winter months. Ms. Mann's uncle, Horace Mann, is known as an educational reformer whose ideology not only ignited the Common School Movement but also created the framework for normal schools offering a standardized normal course program for the formal training of normal teachers in America.

1865

Early antislavery activists, the Free Will Baptists are working in collaboration with several organizations: the United States Bureau of Refugees, Abandoned Lands, and Freedmen (Freedmen's Bureau); United States Christian Commission; American Missionary Association; American Baptist Home Mission Society; Free Will Baptist-Home Mission Society; and the Free Baptist Woman's Missionary Society.

Starting in 1865 and continuing through 1905, twenty-nine educational institutions are established by two Northern Baptist societies:

Timeline

(1) the American Baptist Home Mission Society and (2) the Woman's American Baptist Home Mission Society.

❁ Jefferson County, [West] Virginia, experiences a sustained period of prosperity. By 1865, the county's combined real estate and personal property is assessed at $12,236,982.

❁ Silas Curtis writes a letter to Nathan Cook Brackett in which he states: "[this is] a grand opening for us [the society]—and I will do all in my power to have [the Shenandoah Valley] occupied by our teachers & missionaries. . . . I am anxious we should occupy all that district [in the Shenandoah Valley] those five towns—Harpers Ferry, Martinsburg, Shepherdstown, Charlestown & Berryville—those are historic places."

❁ The Shenandoah Mission is established in Harpers Ferry by the Free Will Baptists-Home Mission Society as its mission center for ongoing operations. Mission teachers arrive to teach literacy skills, character education, and characteristically Christian ethics.

❁ Storer's earliest beginnings were rooted in a mission school network financed by the Free Will Baptist-Home Mission Society under the administration of Nathan Cook Brackett in Harpers Ferry, Charles Town, Martinsburg, Shepherdstown, etc. Mission teachers from Northern states—Maine, New Hampshire, Vermont, and Rhode Island—begin to arrive in Harpers Ferry under the federal protection of the Freemen's Bureau.

❁ After a visit from Rev. Dr. Oren Burbank Cheney, then president of the Maine State Seminary (now Bates College), in 1865 John Storer donates $10,000 to be used to institute a school in the South for freedmen with the proviso that the Free Will Baptists match his donation.

❁ The Free Will Baptists simultaneously open two primary missions in the South. One is established at Beaufort, North Carolina, and the other at Harpers Ferry, West Virginia. The Beaufort site was abandoned after one year in 1866 due to lingering Confederate sympathizers.

❁ Barely one month before the Appomattox surrender, on March 3, the Bureau of Refugees, Freedmen, and Abandoned Lands (Freedmen's Bureau) is granted congressional powers to function as the government's liaison among organized societies offering aid and relief to freed slaves under the supervision of decorated war veteran, Gen. Oliver Otis Howard. The bureau was organized to offer humanitarian aid, quell persistent sectionalism, and educate freedmen in the immediate aftermath of the war.

❁ Rev. Alexander Hatch Morrell cautions Brackett, a zealous administrator, weeks before the mission teacher cohort arrives in Harpers Ferry on November 9: "I hope you will not carry your load of responsibility to disadvantage, as I did, & get sick. O how great a blessing is comfortable health."

❁ The United States Sanitary Commission (USSC) is temporarily housed in the former quarters of the clerk of the Armory superintendent.

This house is commonly called Brackett House since the Brackett family took up residence between 1866 and 1867, although the house was in "bad condition," according to a government inspection report.

⚜ American Freedmen's Union Commission, a nonsectarian organization, is created to provide freedmen with universal education, social uplift, and an environment in which a general aptitude for self-reliance could flourish. By 1866, in an effort to improve the status of freedmen and expand its total operation, the commission had "expended more than $400,000 and supported 760 teachers in the South." It will join forces with other such organizations and charities to alleviate the postwar circumstances of Southern indigents including the more well-off "do-gooders" ostracized by an intransigent Confederacy.

⚜ Just before Thanksgiving, mission teachers arrive by train in Harpers Ferry after a sailing layover in New York during which they heard the fiery reformist preacher George Barrell Cheever, who "was probably the most radical religious abolitionist in America," according to the Christian Ambassador, when the young, impressionable mission teachers heard him. The teachers are received at the station platform by Nathan Cook Brackett. Arriving from New England were Annie S. Dudley (Lewiston), Sarah Jane Foster (Gray), Sabrina L. Gibbs (Wells), and Anna A. Wright, who was a native of Montpelier, Vermont.

⚜ Making notes on the mission teachers' arrival that day was Mary E. Clemmer Ames, wife of Rev. Daniel Ames. Mary Clemmer Ames was well educated and during her lifetime she was the highest paid female journalist, earning $5,000 for her work—solely in 1871—with the Springfield, Massachusetts, *Republican*, the *New York Press*, *The Independent*, and the *Brooklyn Daily Union*.

⚜ After the teachers settle in at Lockwood House, in November, a local Confederate sympathizing newspaper editorial by Charles James Faulkner in the *Martinsburg New Era* publish a veiled threat: "We are much pleased to learn that a large school is soon to be opened for the benefit of the negroes in our midst. We believe the teachers to be ladies from Massachusetts. These ladies will, of course, receive a cordial welcome by the elite of our place, and be at once admitted in to our heartfelt sympathies. We have not yet heard where they are to board, but suppose they will bring their board with them."

⚜ By December 1, Silas Curtis has already designed a mission reporting system. Curtis writes to Brackett, emphatically stating that "Your monthly report to me should look like this . . . [so that] all the financial matter may be kept straight [and] keep all necessary statistics [keeping] people informed & interested in the mission."

Timeline

1866

❀ During the first year, the mission school network, under the regulatory aegis of the Free Will Baptists, has established various schools in different locations and enrolled approximately 2,500 pupils. Brackett's itemized expenditures for four schools included commissaries, kitchen services, blackboard and seats, fuel and lights, rent, travel expenses, board, assistance, stationery, and postage.

❀ The West Virginia Legislature is prompted toward actions leading to a state colored schooling system with an act passed on February 26, 1866, that "provid[ed] for the establishment of colored school in subdistricts containing thirty colored children between the ages of six and twenty-one years." With this act's passage, West Virginia becomes one of the first states in the post–Civil War period to initiate educational opportunities for its "colored" citizens.

❀ Storer College becomes the first formal institution of higher education for Negroes in the State of West Virginia and the first institution of its kind to be recognized by the new thirty-fifth state's legislature as a state Normal Department.

1867

❀ Oren Burbank Cheney, now president of Bates College, travels to Washington to visit his state's Sen. William Pitt Fessenden. During a visit on April 17 with Edwin M. Stanton, United States secretary of war, Cheney discusses abandoned government buildings in Harpers Ferry. Cheney dispatches a note to Brackett, stating, "it is my duty to remain here until I see him [Stanton]; and I propose do so." If Brackett was to respond, Cheney directs him to forward any correspondence in "care of W. Hamlin Esq. Office of the Secretary of the Senate," which was likely based on the advice of Senator Fessenden. Cheney further suggests to Brackett:

> If we can get the lease of the 25 acres and the buildings thereon for a term of years, then we strike for the purchase of the whole government property at the Ferry. We can purchase the property probably at a lower price than any other party, for we want it for the public good—and if we can get possession of it, we can sell it and make a good profit by way of endowing the college. . . . I hope you will not let the business matter at the Ferry be delayed a day. If matters work well here [in Washington], you must close the bargain at almost any price.

❀ Cheney travels on to Harrisburg, Pennsylvania, to meet with George Ball and James Calder. The trio go to a meeting in the national capital with Secretary Simon Cameron in the War Department. During this meeting, it was decided that Calder would approach Governor Boreman of West Virginia to request state aid amounting to $50,000. George Ball returns to his home state of New York to make a request from Gerrit Smith.

⊛ Silas Curtis writes in May: "I am decidedly in favor of a normal school as soon as we can obtain a place without incurring a debt. . . . No colleges nor universities for the Freedmen will be needed for years to come & we had bettern attend to their present needs—I would be glad enough of the property at Harper's Ferry if you consider that a good healthy location & we can get the property. I am in favor getting all the Bureau will let us have— & all we can get—I should hope to secure the 10,000 of Mr. Storer." The Freedmen's Bureau allocates $6,000 for the Freewillers' "Southern enterprise."

⊛ Charles Henry Howard, an editor and publisher and the younger brother of Gen. Oliver Otis Howard, agrees to become a member of the Board of Trustees for Storer College while also a trustee for Howard University. A native of Leeds, Maine, during the war years, C. H. Howard enlisted with the 3rd Maine Infantry and was eventually promoted to colonel by March 1865. Five months later, he became a brevet brigadier general, commander of the United States Colored Troops training facility in Beaufort, South Carolina. He was inspector of schools for the Freedmen's Bureau and received appointments under President James Garfield and subsequently President Chester Arthur after Garfield's assassination.

⊛ Storer College is granted a charter by the West Virginia Legislature as "an institution of learning for the education of youth, without distinction of race or color," although this phrase submitted by the Board of Incorporators on behalf of its Commission for the Promotion of Education in the South was "fiercely debated" between the two legislative branches then located in Wheeling, West Virginia. The institution is simultaneously granted Normal Department status and trained additional teachers for "colored schools" throughout the region.

⊛ Nineteen students enroll "without distinction or race, sex, or religion." Most, if not all, enrolled students were likely graduates of area mission schools, having likely demonstrated mastery of literacy, recitation, elocution, and rote practices.

⊛ John Storer, philanthropist, avowed Whig, and businessman, dies in his home in Sanford, Maine, on October 23 from an "attack of typhoid fever" and prolonged "[g]rief at [Meribah's] death [seven years earlier] and anxiety on account of the war." Although a professed Congregationalist, perhaps one of the last letters composed by Storer before his death indicated his sentiment for the Freewillers: "I knew your people more than sixty years ago, and have traced their progress with wonder and admiration since; and can but exclaim, 'What hath God Wrought!'" After two days of preparations, Free Will Baptist ministers Davis and May officiate at Storer's memorial service and deliver the eulogy on October 25. In his history of Sanford, Maine, Emery describes John Storer as "a genuine contributor to charitable and religious organizations . . . [and d]uring the Civil War no other man in town had the Union cause more at heart."

Timeline

◉ Edward A. Stockman is given a huge responsibility by the Free Will Baptists as chief fund-raiser. Stockman was "in the west," frantically collecting personal notes from friends, family, and supporters of the Free Will Baptists in order to amass the necessary cash capital required by Senator Fessenden as Fessenden was fully committed personally and legally as the guardian executor of John Storer's bequeathal—and its requirement for matching funds.

◉ Peabody Fund director Barnas Sears is consulted as a possible alternative source for funds to match Storer's bequeathal. Sears suggests hiring a New England–trained normal teacher's school graduate named Martha Smith.

◉ Anne (Annie) S. Dudley writes a letter to the Home Mission Society, which is published in the Free Will Baptists' *Morning Star* on October 23, 1867, while dispatched by Brackett to Martinsburg, West Virginia. She taught 115 students in night school and 515 in day and night schools combined. She had an enrollment of 320 students for Sabbath schools. She visited over seven hundred colored families, distributed fifty Bibles, and issued sixty-one other types of books so that students—adults and children—could practice reading skills. Collectively, Dudley's students received from her 11,972 pages on various subjects ranging from conversion to the ills of temperance. Dudley also claimed the following:

I could get no permanent boarding place for nearly two months, (for it would have been a lifelong disgrace for a Virginian to board Yankee teachers, and the rubicon [sic once passed, there could be no return to friends and society, no more than over the walls of caste in India, as public sentiment was then) so I was there alone, boarding myself and teaching day and night, until I had 150 scholars of all ages and complexions from white to black, and of all ages, from four to fifty-five years . . . the blackest child in the school is one of the best scholars I ever saw. They [the scholars] certainly make wonderful progress under the circumstances here in the south.

◉ Dudley, while assigned to Martinsburg, also established a Free Will Baptist church on Raleigh Street. The Dudley [Destiny] Baptist Church will celebrate its 150th anniversary in 2015.

◉ Sarah Jane Foster and Annie Dudley continue to live under threat. Dudley wrote:

The chivalrous students of the Military Institute of Lexington have caused our teachers much trouble. One night a part of them went and demanded one of the scholars, saying, they were going to shoot him. When the teachers could not persuade them to go away, and the rowdies were getting desperate, Miss Harper, one of

the teachers, stepped forward and told them if they shot
Ben they would shoot her first, and with wonderful
courage drove them away, and had them arrested and
taken to court. The matter was hushed up, and Gen.
Lee sent a note of apology to the teachers.

⊛ In November Alexander Hatch Morrell is dispatched by the Home
Mission Society to "take charge of the missionary operations" at the
Shenandoah Mission, while simultaneously Nathan Cook Brackett is
appointed superintendent of schools in Harpers Ferry. As such,
Morrell was also responsible for corresponding with the Morning Star
and the local newspaper, the Berkeley Union in Martinsburg, West
Virginia.

1868

⊛ During a public meeting to which William Lloyd Garrison and
George Whipple are invited as speakers, Garrison publicly claims that
the Free Will Baptists "from the beginning, refused to received slave-
holders into communion," and that regarding the question of slavery,
the Baptists were "prompt[ed] to espouse the doctrine of immediate
emancipation [when] compared to other churches around them," so
that when compared to other like-minded sectarians, the Baptists were
"as light in the midst of darkness. . . . If all other Christian denominations had come up to their level, the chains of the slaves might have

been broken by moral power" alone. Through An Act Providing for the
Sale of Lands, Tenements, and Water Privileges Belonging to the
United States at or Near Harpers Ferry, in the County of Jefferson,
West Virginia, the Department of War granted the Free Will New Light
Baptists temporary usage of the four government buildings—
Lockwood, Anthony, Morrell, and Brackett. With support from Gen.
Oliver Otis Howard, the Free Will Baptists establish Storer College, a
"Hill of Hope," with four bomb-damaged government buildings on
seven acres.

⊛ On January 30, 1868, Nathan Cook Brackett receives correspondence from James Calder in which Calder expresses his concern for
the "terms of contract" and Senator Fessenden's position as "third-
party investor to the Storer estate." Calder accepts the position of
president at Hillsdale College (Michigan) the following year in
1869. Calder's next administrative appointment was as president of
Pennsylvania State College (now Penn State University). Calder
served on the Commission to Promote Education in the South for
its Board of Incorporators, which was directly responsible for the
school's early institutional design.

⊛ Approved in 1867 yet tabled until the legislature's spring term,
Storer College, An Act to Incorporate, dates from March 3, 1868, after
Joseph T. Hoke ascertains a possible conflict of interest and resigns
from the commission for the promotion long enough to cast the

assenting vote for the majority in favor of the Free Will Baptists' "enterprise." By December 15, 1868, the War Department had sold the buildings, valued at $30,000, to the Baptists.

❀ Beginning in 1868, with a donation of $4,000 from the Freedmen's Bureau, the Baptists construct a "three story wooden building 40 x 75 feet containing 34 double rooms" just south of Anthony Memorial Hall with capacity for sixty-eight students. Lincoln Hall, a boys' dormitory, was constructed by "a Union veteran" functioning as "foreman."

1869

❀ James Calder relocates to Hillsdale, Michigan, to assume the presidency of Hillsdale College, which was the Free Will Baptists' collegiate facility in the west.

❀ Storer College's admission standards indicate the degree to which the school's philosophy relies upon the fact that "education" and "morality" are not mutually exclusive. In 1869 and for several years thereafter, admission requires first that students "give satisfactory evidence of a good moral character," including demonstrated proficiencies in reading, spelling, penmanship, geography, and mental arithmetic, before they can be enrolled in the "Regular Course of Study." "The greater the proficiency the student has made in these branches, the better will he be able to master the studies of the Course." If proficiencies were deficient, then students had to enroll first in the Preparatory Program.

1870

❀ Census records indicate that the number of working farms in Jefferson County, West Virginia, increased to 519 with an assessed value for real and personal estates nearing $8 million.

❀ Reverend Morrell and his wife share their Victorian house with twenty to twenty-seven girls whom they chaperoned and boarded while the students attended Storer College.

1871

❀ James Calder, returning to Pennsylvania after the death of Thomas Henry Burrowes, becomes the president of Pennsylvania State College. Calder is responsible for diversifying the student population by convincing the school's all-male Board of Trustees to admit the first women into the school's programs.

1873

❀ Mosher Hall is initially constructed as a girls' dormitory.

❀ During the summer months, Anne Dudley and Martha Stowers chaperone Storer College's vocal ensemble, the Union Chorus, to New York townships and cities—from Buffalo to Utica. The group gave a cappella concerts to solicit donations from interested individuals, groups, and congregations. At one point, Henry Ward Beecher "yielded the pulpit of his church to Dudley for her entreaties." When the tour ended, the ensemble raised $4,000, with an additional donation of

$2,000 from Gerrit Smith. The ensemble is later known as the Harpers Ferry Singers.

1874

⊛ Mary E. Clemmer Ames divorces Rev. Daniel Ames to fulfill her more career-oriented pursuits.

1875

⊛ The aggregate number of students enrolled at Storer is 285.

1876

⊛ Myrtle Hall, Storer's principal girls' dormitory erected just north of Anthony Memorial Hall, is dedicated on May 30. After its completion, Myrtle Hall, named for the Free Will Baptist youth publication, *The Myrtle*, housed the girls' preceptress and matron, boasted thirty-five rooms for students above the basement level and provided in its basement a score of domestic operations, including cooking and laundry facilities.

1877

⊛ John "J. R." Clifford graduates from Storer College.

1878

⊛ Hamilton Hatter graduates from Storer College's Normal /Academic departments and leaves the area to continue his education at Bates College in Maine.

⊛ Brackett is invited to become a member of the Free Will Baptist Foreign Mission Board, a position he would retain for six years. He is also a member of the General Conference Board and the Board of Corporators for the *Morning Star*.

1880

⊛ Twenty-three people now occupy Brackett House: Superintendent Brackett, his wife Louise, their four children (James W., Mary, Celeste E., and Ledru J.); Nathan Brackett's sister, Lura E.; three servants; and thirteen female student boarders.

1881

⊛ The cornerstones for two 42.5-foot-square, two-story complementary annexes are laid on May 31 for Anthony Memorial Hall on the occasion of the school's fourteenth anniversary, making the building 130 feet long. On May 30, the preceding day, the Free Will Baptists' commencement ceremonies are highlighted by two guests: the noted orator, Frederick Douglass, from Washington, D.C., and special prosecutor for the John Brown insurrection, Andrew Hunter, from Charles Town, West Virginia. Douglass had also been a member of the school's first Board of Trustees.

⊛ Sixty female students are boarded in Myrtle Hall. The Free Will Baptist Woman's Missionary Society directly assists fifty students, while the remaining ten receive indirect aid. The woman's society also financed the hall's kitchen, study room, and other day-to-day operations.

Timeline

1882

✸ Rev. Alexander Hatch Morrell donates $5,000 for the construction of the Anthony Hall wing, to be dedicated on May 30, 1882.

✸ Storer's catalogues indicate that international students were enrolled from Liberia, Bermuda, Canada, and Port Republic.

✸ Storer College's longtime trustee, Jonathan McDuffee Brewster, dies on June 2. Brewster was actively engaged with the Executive Committee of the Rhode Island Woman's Suffrage Association as an advocate for women's rights.

✸ Beginning in 1882, Storer's students paid $2 to $5 for schoolbooks. Boarding dormitory students paid 50 cents for an entrance fee in order to defer upkeep and repairs for the "stove, double bedstead, table, and chairs" that furnished each dorm room. Bedding was rented from the school; students could rent "beds complete" ($2 for three months or $3 for eight months). If bedding was returned in good condition, students received a $1 refund.

✸ Students hired out laundry for $1, while fuel costs ran between 25 cents to 50 cents per month. The total expenses students could expect to pay per month ranged from $7.25 to $10.

✸ "[F]or a period of ten years from 1882–1892 the sum of $630 dollars was received annually from the State of W. Va . . . by Storer College."

1883

✸ After moving to Washington, D.C., Mary E. Clemmer Ames marries Edmund Hudson on June 19. Hudson was hailed as the editor of the Army & Navy Register. Their home becomes a literary and social center in the nation's capital. Mary goes on to publish several novels and works of poetry and prose.

1884

✸ From 1884 through 1921, Storer College offers new courses and establishes new departments—Industrial, Biblical, and Musical.

✸ Mary E. Clemmer Ames Hudson dies one year after her marriage to Edmund Hudson.

1888

✸ After graduating from Bates College with a degree in psychology, Hamilton Hatter returns to his West Virginia alma mater. He begins to teach Latin, Greek, and mathematics. Hatter also establishes the Industrial Department of Storer College, using the experience he gained while attending Bates College, where he managed a sawmill between semesters, learning engineering, mechanics, carpentry, and masonry.

✸ Hatter and the students he trains construct the principal building in which the Industrial Department is housed on the campus of Storer

College. Eventually Hatter is appointed as the head superintendent of Bluefield Colored Institute in Bluefield, West Virginia, by the Hon. Virgil A. Lewis. Hatter trains his students for "a man's chance to earn an honest living."

1889

⊛ With financial support from the Woman's Temperance Publication Association, under the combined editorial skills of Gideon A Burgess and John T. Ward, the *Freewill Baptist Cyclopaedia* is published in Chicago.

⊛ On September 29 the Harpers Ferry Free Will Baptist Church cornerstone is set into place. Three years later, in 1892, it is dedicated as the Curtis Memorial Free Will Baptist Chapel in honor of Silas Curtis.

1890

⊛ The Second Morrill Act leads to the establishment of the West Virginia Colored Institute just outside Charleston, the new state capital of West Virginia.

1891

⊛ Kate J. Anthony, the daughter of Rev. Lewis W. Anthony, publishes a "Brief Historical Sketch: Storer College" in the *Morning Star*. The *Star* was the Free Will Baptists' publication.

1892

⊛ Louise Wood Brackett, wife of Nathan Cook Brackett, writes: "General Butler had settled all the perplexing questions in regard to them [freedmen] by the happy application of the word 'contraband,'" for thereafter the circumstances of the freedmen in West[ern] Virginia were improved when the Baptist proceeded with their post-war plan.

1895

⊛ Carter G. Woodson graduates from Douglass High School in Huntington, West Virginia. The Normal Department at Storer College graduates 250 students.

1897

⊛ The Industrial Department is added as a separate formal division of the school with 137 students enrolled.

1898

⊛ Baltimore's Enoch Pratt Library and Mary P. Smith of Nebraska together donate nearly five hundred books to the Roger Williams Library in Anthony Memorial Hall.

⊛ Nathan Cook Brackett steps down as Storer's superintendent after sharp criticism from John "J. R." Clifford. Thereafter, Brackett requests an investigation into "discriminatory" allegations made by Clifford.

Timeline

The investigation by the Board of Trustees would vindicate Brackett the following year.

1899

⊛ Henry Temple McDonald, who was from Michigan, replaces Brackett as the school's principal administrator. He will teach "Biblical literature, Physical Culture, and Oratory." McDonald would retain this position for the next forty-five years until 1944.

1906

⊛ Storer College's campus hosts the first American conference of the Niagara Movement, the antecedent organization for the National Association for the Advancement of Colored People. W. E. B. Du Bois relies on John "J. R." Clifford to act as the local logistical engineer for the event.

1907

⊛ Mary Church Terrell returns to Storer College to lecture on "The Bright Side of a Dark Subject." In 1895, Terrell was the first black woman to be appointed to the District of Columbia Board of Education and was elected the first president of the influential National Association of Colored Women, which on July 14, 1896, convened in Harpers Ferry. The association's motto was "Lifting as We Climb."

⊛ George Wesley Atkinson, former West Virginia governor, addresses students on "The Integrity of the College Student."

1909

⊛ Old Lincoln Hall burns to the ground in April.

1910

⊛ Ella Phillips Stewart, a Berryville, Virginia, native and purported to be among the first Negro pharmacists in the country, graduates from Storer College.

⊛ Dr. Nathan Cook Brackett dies and is buried in "his adopted state" in the Harper Cemetery, located behind Lockwood House and just above the hill behind the Gothic style St. Peter's Roman Catholic Church, built in 1833.

⊛ The construction of New Lincoln Hall is completed in October. The new hall is rededicated later as Brackett Hall. It is a 3.5-story limestone building with nine windows on the building's frontage and includes a partial subterranean elevation.

1914

⊛ A native of Parkersburg, West Virginia, Mary Peyton Dyson graduates from Storer for a second time after completing the Normal Department program in 1908.

1918

⚘ Congressman L. C. Dyer contacts John R. Shillady, secretary of the National Association of Colored People, requesting recent lynching data from the South in support of the AntiLynching Bill.

⚘ Myrtle Hall is converted to a men's dormitory. Between 1920 and 1930, the hall is renamed Mosher Hall.

1920

⚘ Donald "The Little Giant of Jazz" Redman graduates from Storer College. A famous arranger, orchestrator, and composer, Redman eventually takes his own orchestra to Europe and appears with Max Fleisher's "Betty Boop" in cartoon imagery.

⚘ President McDonald promotes the school by designing a brochure titled "Storer College Gives You Welcome." McDonald was "sending letters to Africa, [as well as] South America and widely over the United States."

1921

⚘ Carter G. Woodson, a former teacher in West Virginia's "colored schools" who taught at Winona in Fayette County, is ultimately persuaded to accept the position of principal administrator for Douglass High School in Cabell County. He was the founder of the *Journal of Negro History* in 1921, and wrote that in order to "pro-

claim the power of education as the great leverage by which the recently emancipated race could toil up to a position of recognition in this republic," institutions established during the post–Civil War period organized curricula for an essential "teaching force" that "enabled the Negroes to help themselves." Woodson also noted "the successful work being accomplished there [at Storer College] under the direction of Dr. N. C. Brackett—[since it was] the only effort for secondary education for Negroes in the State" until the 1890 Morrill Act.

⚘ Storer College is granted junior collegiate status.

1924

⚘ Madison Spenser Briscoe graduates from Storer College.

1925

⚘ McDonald is confronted with the issue of black teachers and white teachers at Storer College, an issue that had long been a topic of debate and maintained as a focus of attention by W. E. B. Du Bois, Kelly Miller, J. R. Clifford, and others.

1926

⚘ The state legislature's annual contribution increases to slightly over $6,000, yet this sum "did not even cover half the salaries of the faculty and administration."

◉ McDonald joins other presidents of Baptist schools for "colored youth" at an Atlanta conference designed to consider the widespread funding situation. The conference agrees on a joint five-year fund-raising drive with a goal of $5 million to $6 million. Storer's needs were nearing $400,000. The joint operation is quashed by the American Baptist Home Mission Society, which believed the organization was already overextended.

1927

◉ Anthony Memorial Hall is damaged by fire on October 24, with estimates for repairs nearing $60,000. The hall would again suffer fire damage in 1937 and 1939.

1928

◉ A special meeting of the Board of Trustees is arranged to make a final decision for the school: (1) "to keep the school's present Baptist affiliation with such state aid as could be had or (2) "to place the college under state control." The second idea was passed. Dr. Alfred Williams Anthony, a member of the Board of Trustees and son of founding agent, Lewis W. Anthony, discusses with other Baptist officials the possibility of removing McDonald.

1929

◉ The Great Depression takes a foothold in America on September 4. When the stock market ultimately crashes on October 29, the unemployment rate soars to over 600 percent.

1931

◉ Dr. Madison Spencer Briscoe accepts a faculty position at Storer College. Briscoe lives in Harpers Ferry and commutes to Washington, D.C., to teach in the School of Medicine at Howard University.

1932

◉ The West Virginia Legislature reduces its financial support from $17,500 to $12,000.

1933

◉ McDonald, in his annual report, states that the situation at Storer is grim. He notes: "We secured some financial assistance from alumni and friends, we made liberal scholarship grants, whenever possible and we created jobs, wherever there was the slightest excuse" to help students in need. McDonald then added one final line that sums up the state of the nation, but highlights the trials faced by blacks, the least empowered segment of society: "An impoverished peoples cannot send their sons and daughters to college."

1936

◉ The first four-year class graduates from Storer College in Harpers Ferry.

◉ Louise Wood Brackett dies in Brackett House, where she lived alone in a second-floor apartment for twenty-six years after the death of her husband, Rev. Dr. Nathan Cook Brackett, in 1910.

1940

⊛ Permelia Eastman Cook Hall is added to the campus. The building is named in honor of its principal donor, who contributed $15,000.

1941

⊛ Lockwood House is now used as an apartment building for faculty.

⊛ The Board of Trustees creates a new position, dean of instruction, which eliminates the two positions dean of men and dean of women.

1942

⊛ Hamilton H. Hatter, a venerable graduate of Storer College hailed throughout West Virginia for his dedication to quality education and the retired principal of Bluefield State Colored Institute, dies on September 21. Hatter, born in Jefferson County, was one of the first blacks to be nominated for political ballot for the West Virginia House of Representatives.

⊛ McDonald resigns as the school's treasurer. Later, he left both the Finance and Executive committees.

1943

⊛ By the end of the school term, President McDonald "had been relieved of most of his duties" and therefore resigns.

1944

⊛ The McDonalds move from Anthony Hall to Brackett Hall, where Mrs. McDonald remains until the school's closure in 1955.

⊛ Dr. Richard Ishmael McKinney is selected by the Board of Trustees as McDonald's successor. The eminently qualified McKinney was a graduate of Morehouse, Andover Newton Theological Seminary, and earned a Ph.D. from Yale University. He came to Storer College after having been the dean of the School of Religion at Virginia Union University. The first night McKinney arrived in the ferry town, he was welcomed by a burning cross on his front lawn. Before accepting the administrative position, McKinney knew full well he would be fighting the tide of local sentiment, yet he "began his administration full of optimism and ambitiously set to work to bring [the school] up to the standards of the modern four-year college."

1945

⊛ Storer College is awarded senior collegiate status.

⊛ McKinney establishes a NAACP chapter and forms a Student Government Association.

1946

⊛ West Virginia accredits Storer's B.A. in elementary education, as well as the English, home economics, science, and social science sections of its Secondary Education division.

Timeline

⊛ McKinney increases the number of Negro faculty and even initiates correspondence with Nnamdi "Zik" Azikiwe in Nigeria.

1947

⊛ A science building is constructed since "more and more students were asking for premedical courses." McKinney continues to work on state and regional accreditations.

⊛ McKinney invites Nnamdi "Zik" Azikiwe to be the commencement speaker. "Zik" delivers a rallying cry to activism through social leadership and democratic principles. Storer College conferred upon "Zik" one of only two honorary degrees bestowed by the institution during its operation.

⊛ Madison Spencer Briscoe helps McKinney get the Pre-Medic Program off the ground and begins teaching advanced sciences: bacteriology, parasitology, etc.

1948

⊛ Despite McKinney's best efforts, the school was unable to fully qualify for accreditation since South Central accreditation required a mandatory endowment of $100,000, which would restrict Storer's membership.

1949

⊛ The school bulletin articulates the joint vision of its president and faculty in a series of ten objectives.

⊛ The Executive Committee votes to increase tuition from $100 to $120, yet votes to reduce annual fees from $50 to $40, an odd inversion of fiscal policy, did not resonate with President McKinney.

⊛ McKinney offers his resignation, which the board refuses to accept and he is temporarily reinstated, although McKinney was aware that at least one vocal enemy among its members was impugning his authority.

1950

⊛ In April at the board meeting, McKinney again tenders his resignation. He leaves after the commencement ceremony in May to accept a position at Morgan State College in Baltimore, where he would remain until his retirement.

⊛ During the fall, Storer College is managed for two years by an Interim Administrative Committee, chaired by Leroy Dennis Johnson, a faculty member and dean of men.

1952

⊛ In May, Rev. Leonard Earl Terrell is selected to manage the school's interests. The school year begins with a deficit of near $12,000 with enrollment projections declining. Terrell is the last principal administrator in the history of the school.

⊛ School property begins to be sold. The school's vice-president "recommended that a committee be formed to look into the sale of any college property not expected to be used in the future development."

1953

⊛ "As early as February, the Board of Trustees was already beginning to seriously discuss the future of Storer."

⊛ During the fall term, the deficit for that school year was $9,019 and approximately $10,000 was due on unpaid bills.

1954

⊛ On May 19, 1954, the U.S. Supreme Court's decision to desegregate public schools projects the closure of Storer College in Harpers Ferry.

⊛ The Executive Board recommends to the Board of Trustees that the college suspend operations for the 1954–55 school year.

⊛ Storer alumni begin a "Save Storer" campaign, which meets with some early success. The alumni "raised $5,000 for scholarship for West Virginia students, and recruited more students than Storer had had for the previous two years."

1955

⊛ Terrell submits his resignation in April. The school's debt load is now at $35,000, and $16,000 is needed for the next school term.

⊛ With W. E. B. Du Bois's closing commencement speech, Storer College confers it last degrees to graduates on Camp Hill in the wake of *Brown vs. Board of Education*, Topeka, Kansas.

1958

⊛ The board and its convention circulate a request for proposals designed to solicit aid and support.

⊛ To reinstate Storer College's operation, on September 11, Alderson-Broaddus College in Phillipi, West Virginia, proposes an institutional merger.

⊛ The national officers and the bishops for the African Methodist Episcopal Zion Church (AMEZC) arrange for an all-day conference to put together a tentative proposal for consideration by the Storer College Board of Trustee. The AMEZC understood proposals were to be submitted for "the purpose of continuing the operation and education purposes" of Storer College. The AMEZC developed "procedures for negotiations," ad hoc committees, assigned representatives, and ultimately designed an eight-point proposal.

⊛ Storer College's Board of Trustees had two separate proposals from which to choose in order to maintain the school's operations.

⊛ The Board of Trustees votes to accept the proposal from Alderson-Broaddus and liquidate Storer's assets. Two board members and Storer graduates—Mary Peyton Dyson and Madison Spencer Briscoe—were decidedly against liquidating the school's assets and closing down the campus.

Timeline

1959

⊛ On February 11, Dyson and Briscoe file a "Motion for Preliminary Injunction" in the United States District Court for the District of Columbia to prevent the Special Committee appointed by Clarence Cranford from beginning the liquidation of Storer's assets.

⊛ Washington's District Court remanded the case back to West Virginia. Once that happened, Dyson and Briscoe knew it was a foregone conclusion that the school would be closed since the "township did not want the colored school in the first place."

⊛ Dyson and Briscoe did not recover their legal costs, which were "in excess of $3,000.00 exclusive of costs" incurred by their legal counsel during the course of legal preparation and investigation. Once the case was moved to West Virginia, Storer's future was sealed.

1960

⊛ The Storer College campus was incorporated as part of the Harpers Ferry National Historical Park under the supervision of the National Park Service Division of the United States Department of the Interior.

1963

⊛ The northeast regional director of the National Park Service proposes that Storer College should be understood in a way that is meaningfully situated "against the broader history of the period."

⊛ The National Park Service takes control of the campus and grounds.

⊛ Mosher Hall, a two-story stone building that was formerly Myrtle Hall, is razed by the National Park Service.

1999

⊛ Dr. Richard Ishmael McKinney living in Baltimore, Maryland and a former Storer College President, indicates his interest and willingness to represent Storer College on the Virginia Polytechnic & State University dissertation committee. Dr. Houston G. Brooks Jr., a Storer graduate, agrees to also function as a doctoral coaching mentor—as McKinney—for Dawne Raines Burke through the dissertation's completion.

2000

⊛ As attorney Henry Morrow had been a member of the Special Committee assembled by Storer's Board of Trustees, he was asked about the school's closure in 1955. Morrow responded, "I was brought on to that committee, for no other reason, than to administer the liquidation of the school and its assets."

Storer College

*S*torer College began during a pivotal juncture in American history. At the spectacular confluence of the Potomac and Shenandoah Rivers, in Harpers Ferry, West Virginia, the great question of slavery and the future of the Union was framed in one of the defining moments of the Republic. John Brown's audacious 1859 raid on Hall's Rifle Works and the federal arsenal at Harpers Ferry galvanized public opinion on the "slave question." The federal arsenal that Brown targeted, and its setting at the meeting of great rivers, were forever seared into the collective memory of the nation, poignant reminders of the deep divisions that separated competing visions for the country. Brown's violent attempt at formenting a slave insurrection failed, but the abolitionist message he bore survived him, and in fact only became stronger after his execution.

Southeastern panoramic view of the confluence of the Potomac and Shenandoah rivers in Harpers Ferry, West Virginia.

Soon after the Civil War ended, almost at the very site of Brown's attack, Harpers Ferry became once again an important location of historic change. In 1867, Storer College, one of the first integrated schools in the United States, opened its doors to students. The importance of the location and the historical mission of Storer College stood as an answer to the rhetorical question asked by Frederick Douglass, "Was John Brown's raid a success?"

The college was formed from several mission schools founded around 1865, the result of the efforts of a group of committed philanthropists. In the wake of the Civil War, just after the hostilities ended, large-scale philanthropic efforts were undertaken by individuals and denominational groups, as well as state and federal supporters of their endeavors. Their efforts were subsequently responsible for giving rise to a Negro College Movement, which established institutions for providing freed

JOHN BROWN'S
STRONGHOLD AT
HARPERS FERRY.
OCTOBER 17-18, 1859.

Federal Arsenal Engine House and John Brown's 1859 refuge fort

slaves and later other African Americans with advanced educational degrees. These farsighted reformers attempted to reshape racial relations in the wake of the devastating attrition of the Civil War, according to the ethical, religious, and moral duties that they believed were the responsibilities of the prosperous. Among these efforts, several themes are evident. The end of factional fighting, the drive to reform, and a general desire to reforge the conscience of the nation are pervasive elements in many of the projects that were undertaken as a part of this philanthropic effort.

Storer College was historically significant for its insistence on the principles of inclusion and integration. In 1867, Storer was granted a charter by the West Virginia Legislature as "an institution of learning for the education of youth, without distinction of race or color," although the qualifying phrase "without distinction of race or color" was fiercely debated between the two legislative houses. Those in

favor of the school's charter likely believed that educational development was essential for the state's entire population, beneficial for all, including the state's minority populations. Remaining pockets of Confederate sympathizers were hostile to the postwar social reforms and opposed the new school. Circumstances ultimately favored the institution, however, and for the next ninety years, Storer distinguished itself by its important role in the development of higher education for African Americans. In its early years, Storer was the only school in the entire region where blacks could be educated and became the first college for blacks in West Virginia.

Storer College's role as a reforming educational institution and its symbolic importance to the ultimate success of abolitionist goals, positioned the school nicely as a site for important public speeches on racial issues. On May 30, 1881, for example, on the occasion of Storer's fourteenth anniversary, Frederick Douglass delivered an unforgettable commencement address on the legacy of John Brown's raid some twenty years earlier. Douglass said, "If John Brown did not end the war that ended slavery, he did at least begin the war that ended slavery . . . not Carolina, but Virginia, not Fort Sumter, but Harpers Ferry, and the arsenal, not Colonel Anderson, but John Brown, began the war that ended American slavery and made this a free Republic."

As a groundbreaking institution, it seems that much was expected of Storer, both from its own administrators and from the public. The unique setting of Storer made it a portentous site for African American civil rights to be advanced, and it is in this light that Storer College made a niche for itself in the struggle for equality. In 1906, Storer's campus hosted the first American conference of the Niagara Movement, the antecedent organization for the National Association for the Advancement of Colored People (NAACP).

Over the years, Storer's educational mission developed from its missionary school beginnings to its final years as a four-year college. The college was known for its academics, its athletic teams, and its music ensembles. The college proudly lists a wide variety of specialized educational programs, from

The 1906 Second Niagara Conference Delegation assembles outside Anthony Hall (Mather Training Center) on the Storer College campus.

normal school offerings and industrial arts programs to religious and musical training, to rigorous scientific curricula. One of the basic foundations of an education at Storer was the quality of "self-dependence," and it is quite apparent that Storer graduates served the region with honor. Storer also created a much wider reputation than its size and funding would suggest through its ambitious and successful efforts to find a place on campus for African students, one of whom

William Edward Burghardt (W.E.B.) Du Bois, a Niagara Movement Founder.

later became the the first elected president of Federation Nigeria. Storer College also presented many public lectures from prominent speakers of the day as a way to enhance the institution's influence.

Ironically, Storer College, founded on integrationist principles, met its demise as a degree-granting institution in the wake of the landmark 1954 Supreme Court decision, *Brown v. The Board of Education of Topeka, Kansas.* While many historically black colleges continued on after the tradition of "separate but equal" ended, Storer College was faced with monetary struggles and an unsympathetic state legislature. The college therefore opted to close its doors, with defenders of the decision declaring that its historic mission of integrated education was fulfilled.

Beginnings
The Setting and Its Historical Context

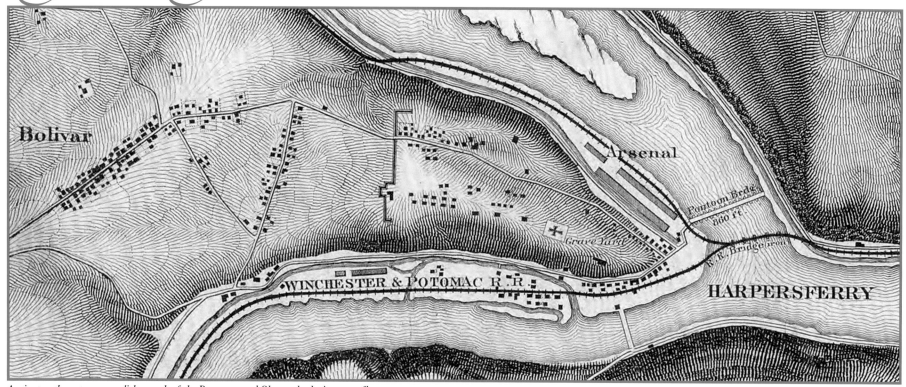

A nineteenth-century map lithograph of the Potomac and Shenandoah rivers confluence

SETTING: THE VIRGINIAS BEFORE FREE WILL BAPTISTS AND ORGANIZED PHILANTHROPY

Historically, Virginia had always possessed two distinct personalities based on the differing ways of life of its people. The first was rooted in the folkways of the eastern part of the state and its seacoast, often associated with the antebellum South. This character was defined by colonialism, tobacco cultivation, plantation aristocracy, leisured hunting, high culture, and the replication of an idealized European civilization based on privilege. Virginia's second regional identity, quite the opposite, is embodied in the mountainous western frontier. This other Virginia, the Appalachian, is linked with agrarianism, animal husbandry, mountain traditions amid arduous terrain, independence, hunting for necessity, and isolation.

The dichotomy of identity in a single state was long the substance of internal conflicts, and played a great role in an issue as important as education. In the antebellum era (the period just prior to the onset of the Civil War), Virginia was comprised of four districts: Trans-Allegheny (later, Western), Valley, Blue Ridge (later, Piedmont), and Tidewater. Undeniably, there emerged from the four Virginia districts two distinct divisions, based largely upon the state's geography: the Trans-Allegheny and Valley districts made up the western division, with the Blue Ridge and Tidewater districts comprising the eastern division. The geographical remoteness between the divisions spurred social, economic, and political isolation. The western section was separated from the more populous east by geography and social difference, and developed its own ways of dealing with its perceived issues. This

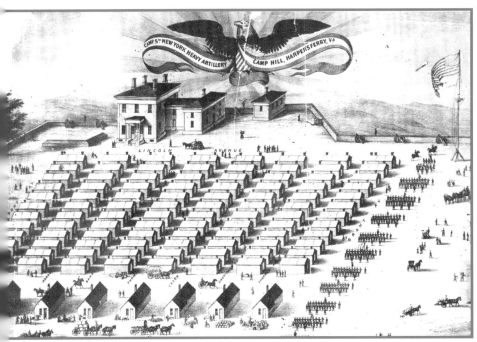

The logistical design for troops on Camp Hill, the future site of Storer College, in 1861

disjunction from the eastern mainstream led to divisive actions in the western section, followed ultimately by proactive organizations politically and otherwise.

Trilateral instability—socially, economically, and politically—over education between the two divisions of Virginia, as well as the schism that resulted from Virginia's secession during the Civil War, led to the western division's statehood.

Although the earliest schools in the western division could in no way compare to eastern counterparts in terms of opulence and support, they still served an important function. They were an indication that even in the wilderness, even along the frontier, Virginians realized that in order to fully participate in the operation of state government, education would equip them for the political and social struggles that lay ahead. Control of such education, however, rested mainly with the Virginia General Assembly. What did it think about educating citizens? Into what populations was it willing or unwilling to extend the benefits of education—whites, free coloreds, or freedmen? Education was viewed by the Western Virginians as the means by which to put all Virginians on equal footing. It was generally seen as the best means of developing an equitable and unified system of representation. This was especially important in the less affluent western portion of the state, and seen by that population as the tool to lead the state toward social change and political equity, therefore contributing to the economic welfare of its citizens as a whole.

Historical Context

Free Will Baptists, the Home Mission Society, and the Bureau of Refugees, Abandoned Lands, and Freedmen

Prewar sectionalism and the corresponding divisive circumstances after the Civil War are the defining historical realities from which Storer College emerged. It was in this divisive atmosphere in Virginia that the Free Will Baptists' mission teachers, by order of their Home Mission Society and coordinated through the American Missionary Association, eventually migrated to Harpers Ferry. There, they were to put into effect their own educational plan in order to help bridge this great divide between Virginia's two natures in the Shenandoah Valley, a gulf that was a microcosm of that which split the nation as a whole.

To be fully understood and appreciated, the history of Storer College must be viewed against a larger postwar context in which numerous and varied schools were organized on behalf of emancipated slaves, known as freedmen after the war. Collectively, these schools comprised the Negro College Movement, a postwar response to destruction, deprivation, confusion, and emancipation.

Benjamin Randal, the eighteenth-century Free Will Baptist founder

The Free Will Baptists and several similar philanthropic organizations and individuals were particularly conscious of escalating illiteracy rates among Negroes. Just over forty years before the first Free Will Baptists arrived in Virginia, in 1861, the State of Virginia had enacted several laws, as was common throughout the South, to prevent the education of slaves. In 1819, for example, two laws were created in Virginia to deter benevolent whites from associating with blacks for the purpose of teaching slaves to read. The first law made localized assemblage of Negro slaves for the purpose of instruction unlawful. Those white citizens who were successfully prosecuted for teaching slaves to read were imprisoned or fined—or sometimes both. In such cases, the Negroes were publicly lashed. By 1838, Virginia made out-of-state educational pursuits by free Negroes a civil offense. Free Negroes were banished, and therefore, forfeited Virginia residency if they left the state to become educated citizens. Given this background, it is easy to understand why and how the development of education for freed slaves in the Virginias was a particularly thorny issue. The Free Will Baptisits became a leading force in promoting education for freedmen in the postwar years.

The Free Will Baptists were a New England denomination, with the first church established in 1770 in New Durham, New Hampshire, by Benjamin Randal, a George Whitefield convert. By the nineteenth century, the ecclesiastical concentration of the Free Will Baptist denomination had expanded to include Maine, Rhode Island, Vermont, and various points west and south.

Whitefield was an eighteenth-century British evangelist associated with the religious revival of the Second Great Awakening and influenced by the Age of Enlightenment. He made several trips from England to colonial America, which was indeed deeply influenced as a result of such evangelical efforts to a greater sense of moral principle and social obligation. Thus, through his conversion of Benjamin Randal, George Whitefield became the model for the evangelical fervor and missionary zeal that were closely connected with the Free Will Baptists.

The Free Will Baptists were held in high regard by prominent abolitionists like William Lloyd Garrison. In 1868, Garrison claimed that the Free Will Baptists "from the beginning, refused to receive slave-holders into communion." This distinguished the denomination from others that publicly endorsed gradual emancipation, voluntary emancipation, or recolonization approaches to transport slaves back to their native continents and islands of origin. When Garrison's American Anti-Slavery Society was organized in 1833, the sectarians were philosophically, theologically, and socially allied with Garrison against institutionalized slavery.

They began to work with other organizations and philanthropists to formulate plans for improving the social welfare of southern Negroes by educating slaves once the war ended. The denomination fervently believed that the demise of both foreign and domestic institutionalized slavery was destined to become the main goal of the war. The Free Will Baptists had considerable support from Northern blacks, and promised to offer education to former slaves in the South. The denomination,

"[Free Will Baptists] [were] prompt[ed] to espouse the doctrine of immediate emancipation [when] compared to other churches around them."

William Lloyd Garrison

"If all other Christian denominations had come up to their level, the chains of the slaves might have been broken by moral power."

–*William Lloyd Garrison*

therefore, simultaneously opened two primary missions: one in Beaufort, North Carolina, and the other in Harpers Ferry, West Virginia when the war came to an end.

By the end of the Civil War, the need for a reorganized system of education that included Negroes became overwhelmingly evident to reform-minded individuals and organizations. Four million freed slaves, war refugees, and public indigents lived in the South, and among them illiteracy rates were astounding. In an effort to relieve the plight of a number of these freedmen, the Free Will Baptist denomination had already devised a incremental plan of education and founded several mission schools for that purpose throughout the Shenandoah Valley. The Free

Day-to-day operations by federal troops on Camp Hill, 1862

Will Baptists had long recognized that denial of literacy and education had been methods of subjugation, and they had specific plans to remedy the situation.

Free Will Baptist missionaries readily relocated to the valley, not only to establish the schools but also to organize the Shenandoah Mission center in Harper's Ferry. After a period of time, however, their educational plan demanded further progress. A high school was

planned, but the ultimate goal was to establish a college for Negroes in the South. This missionary initiative eventually led to the establishment of Storer College, which further developed incrementally. The legacy of reform from this early missionary impulse remained in the ongoing development of Storer. First it was a mission school, intended to provide elementary education. Next, Storer became a normal school to train teachers of the traditional academic canon of the three R's. Its mission then expanded to encompass musical, biblical, and industrial departments. Finally, the school joined the collegiate ranks, first as a junior college, and then as a degree-granting undergraduate institution.

In 1867, during the post–Civil War philanthropic era that gave rise to the Negro College Movement, Storer College was established by the Free Will Baptist denomination in Lockwood House on Camp Hill, in Harpers Ferry, West Virginia, an outgrowth of the mission school that had existed there since 1865.

Since the end of the war, the Free Will Baptists, early antislavery activists, worked in collaboration with a number of agencies. Among these were the Bureau of Refugees, Abandoned Lands, and Freedmen, United States Christian Commission, American Missionary Association, American Baptist Home Mission Society, [Free Will Baptist] Home Mission Society, and the Free Baptist Woman's Missionary Society. Their broad aim was to educate freedmen in Southern states. In these formative years, they had established an entire network of mission schools throughout the Shenandoah Valley. Their Home Mission Society had in this manner invested in the moral, social, and educational uplifting of a number of freedmen.

The Freedmen's Bureau

Alongside the various sectarian groups that provided humanitarian aid, a government agency was also organized to assist relief efforts. On March 3, 1865—barely a month before the Confederate Army surrendered at Appomattox—the Bureau of Refugees, Freedmen, and Abandoned Lands (also termed, the Freedmen's Bureau) was granted congressional powers to function as the government's liaison among organized societies offering aid and relief to freed slaves. During the postwar period 1865–1870, the Freedman's Bureau, under the leadership of decorated war veteran General Oliver Otis Howard, worked to instill in the nation a sense of urgency for offering humanitarian aid, quelling persistent sectionalism, and educating freedmen. Although it was all but defunct by 1870, in its five-year existence, the bureau reinstated civil order, cultivated mutual trust, and enforced public policies in townships where Confederate hostilities remained. The bureau eventually assumed the role of broker, as it negotiated contracts for labor, education, and agriculture as an exercise of the administrative powers with which it had been endowed by Congress through the Secretary of War.

The role of the Freedmen's Bureau contributed to an increasing attrition rate among benevolent societies, associations, and organizations that arrived in the South in the war's aftermath. Ten years after the establishment of the Freedmen's Bureau, few societies, organizations, and associations remained in the South to execute this ongoing work. However, four benevolent societies did remain constant, doubling rather than reducing their efforts to improve education: the American Missionary Association (Congregationalist); the Freedmen's Aid Society (Methodist Episcopal); the American Baptist Home

Mission Society (Baptist); and the Committee on Missions to Freedmen (Presbyterian). Their persistence proved vital.

During the postwar period, a system of formalized education was instituted in the South by Northerners accepting this shared responsibility. As they descended into the South, such northerners were truly surprised by the intensity of lingering Confederate sympathies, most easily recognized in border states. In order to help reduce such sympathies and return social unity to the region, a system was concurrently developed to initiate educational instruction, instill moral virtue, and create opportunities for social civility and political advancement among freedmen. Under the direction of civil, martial, and denominational representatives, this system was conceived as a "Southern experiment" that flourished primarily between 1865 and 1910.

Denominational Collaboration: Three Crucial Societies

In the example the Free Will Baptists provided, when compared to other denominations, the Baptists were "as light in the midst of darkness," noted Garrison. "If all other Christian denominations had come up to their level," he further asserted, "the chains of the slaves might have been broken by moral power" alone. Garrison was not the only abolitionist to recognize the Free Will Baptists as leading proponents of ending slavery and helping former slaves.

George Whipple, an ardent abolitionist, also held the Free Will Baptists in high regard. Under his leadership, the American Missionary

Association made its greatest strides. Whipple worked directly with the Baptists to arrange commissions and transportation routes for mission personnel, configure logistics, create recruitment opportunities, and provide financial subsidies and political intelligence to reinforce the cause. It is not surprising, then, that the American Missionary Association under his direction subsequently entered into contract with the Free Will Baptists. The latter group had demonstrated the sort of moral resolution, intellectual resilience, and social dedication that assured their place at the forefront of early abolitionist organizations.

With their elevated sense of moral resolution, the Free Will Baptists devised an educational plan, guided by Whipple's input and intelligence, to extend efforts directly into the South. The result was the Shenandoah Mission in Harpers Ferry, a collaborative effort among three crucial denominational societies: the Free Will Baptist Home Mission Society, the Anti-Slavery Society, and the Free Baptist Woman's Missionary Society. After emancipation, however, the Anti-Slavery Society channeled its resources to the Home Mission Society.

Home Mission Society (1834)

On July 31, 1834, the Free Will Baptist Home Mission Society was organized in Dover, New Hampshire, when "ten men became life members by paying $15 each, and four women became honorary members by paying $10 each." Because the Free Will Baptist recognized women early as viable contributors, they were integrated into the decision-making processes.

Although the society began with only $190 in its treasury, by September 1, 1888, it had generated $294,564 in revenue to finance its home mission investments.

Anti-Slavery Society (1843)

In 1843, the Free Will Baptist Anti-Slavery Society was organized in New Hampshire. To this end, the Free Will Baptists were constant and unflagging in their adamant abolitionist position. As the moral voice of the new society, Benjamin Randal wrote a statement of the society's aims, which included: self-government, independence, democracy, and the free will to exercise all. These strongly resonated with various aspects of the Free Will Baptist enterprise. The following year, in 1844, a denominational schism resulted when Baptist slaveholders were openly confronted during a large convention of the Baptists. As a result, the Baptist denomination proper was divided thereafter into Northern and Southern conventions, a schism that lasted until 1911. At a time when the chief argument for the continuation of slavery most inflamed and consumed the American republic, the Free Will Baptists had taken "a bold and unflinching stance on the side of freedom."

Women's Missionary Society (1847)

With a strong conviction to adhere to church authority and acknowledge the "universal call to mankind" and therefore all humanity, the Free Will Baptist women in 1847 formed their own organization to support and finance both foreign and domestic missions. At the triennial Free Will Baptist General Conference, held in Sutton, Vermont, the denomination's women organized what was initially called the Free Baptist Female Mission Society, but would in 1865 become the Free Baptist Female Systematic Beneficence Society.

After twenty years of activity, "change[s] of circumstances," reduced attendance at meetings, and decreased funding finally put an end to the society's "good and effective service." Although divested of its responsibility, the society was never fully dissolved. Its members remained in contact with the hope of revitalizing it to benefit that portion of their membership involved in mission work. In 1873, the society reactivated in order "to take advanced ground, select and support their own missionaries." At a meeting at Sandwich, New Hampshire, on June 11, 1873, a constitution was formed. Ten years later, on January 26, 1883, the society was chartered by the New Hampshire Legislature, resulting in 250 auxiliaries with over six thousand members, to direct foreign and domestic operations. The society's official history, written by Margaret H. Hutchins Hills, states that throughout its duration, the society "carefully remembered" Harpers Ferry, West Virginia. It routinely contributed to Storer's development, and sponsored and paid the salaries of several teachers.

Without the collaboration of these three denominational societies, the institution of mission schools and consequently the development of Storer College might not have been possible, particularly when consideration is given to the inordinate social, economic, and political circumstances that challenged nineteenth-century Americans.

The Founding of Storer

The eventual creation of Storer College was made possible by an unlikely and dramatic series of events. The first of these was a dispute over runaway slaves that set an 1861 legal precedent. This precedent was set by General Benjamin F. "Peg Leg" Franklin Butler at Fortress Monroe, in the eastern part of the state, in the early days of the Civil War. Three slaves, named Shepard Mallory, Frank Baker, and James Townsend, were temporarily released from work at a Hampton plantation by their owner, General Charles K. Mallory, on May 23, 1861. They were sent to reinforce a construction project for a Confederate battery. However, they quickly bypassed the construction site, crossed the Chesapeake Bay from Sewall's Point near Hampton, and headed for the peninsula's stronghold, Fortress Monroe, located at the confluence of the York and James rivers. Reaching Fortress Monroe without incident, the slaves approached Butler's picket guards, whom he had posted on May 22 when he officially assumed command. In exchange for a full account of their actions to General Butler, who was the commander of the Department of Virginia, the slaves were given provisional refuge for the night.

The following morning, Butler heard appeals from all three slaves, who "represented that they were about to be sent South [to Florida], and hence sought protection" with Union forces. After listening to the slaves' pro-Unionist pleas, Butler's staff officer notified him that an unfurled truce flag had been hoisted just outside the fort by Confederate Major John B. Cary. The mayor begged for an audience with the commanding general on behalf of Colonel Mallory.

Benjamin F. "Peg-Leg" Butler

Fortress Monroe cannon guns organized for action during the war years in 1861

the Old Dominion in direct violation of the United States government and that, therefore, she was a "foreign body" in due process of federal occupation under direct orders from the Union's commander-in-chief, the US president. Butler was reluctant or unwilling, therefore, to comply with the 1850 Fugitive Slave Act, which gave legal sanction to "slave owners to enter other states to capture and reclaim their property." The Fugitive Slave Act was interpreted by the Confederates to mean that they had the right to storm Fortress Monroe in order to "capture and reclaim their property" under any circumstances.

Acting as legal proxy for Colonel Charles K. Mallory, Cary insisted that Butler return Mallory's "property." Butler promptly refused, claiming that he was "under no constitutional obligations" to acknowledge Mallory's request. The general cited four basic reasons for his position. First, during the preceding week, on May 17, Virginia seceded from the Union; secondly, they had declared state sovereignty; thirdly, they had abrogated the United States Constitution; and lastly, they had formed a coalition with other Confederation States.

To Butler, such actions were verifiable evidence of enemy collusion. The general went on to assert that Virginia's actions subsequently placed

Butler's understanding of American wartime laws also dictated that "all rights of property of whatever kind, will be held inviolate, subject only to the laws of the United States." Virginia, however, seceded from the United States in direct opposition to the laws of the land, as Butler knew and understood them.

An early nineteenth-century rendition of a slave pleading for social and moral consideration as he poses the question: "Am I not a man and a brother?"

Therefore, he held that the rebellious Virginians had no recourse to the act.

Collectively, the actions of the fugitive threesome and General Butler's response to Cary prompted a slave exodus that grew exponentially into a major factor in battle operations during 1861. Slaves and refugees, hearing that they would not be returned to their owners, began to arrive at the Union camp in increasing numbers seeking food, shelter, and sanctuary. However, this mass of displaced slaves raised substantive questions for which Butler was ill prepared, and worsened his circumstances as commander.

Butler repeatedly dispatched messengers to the War Department requesting an official response to the situation at the fort, but his inquiries were deflected. Butler queried Simon Cameron in the War Department concerning possible military actions. He also solicited responses from political officials. This call for assistance fell on the deaf ears of his Washington superiors for some time, but Butler's requests for support—military, political, and

Main entrance to Fortress Monroe during the Civil War with unfurled American flag

social—further incited the slave influx. Clearly, the incident at Fortress Monroe had far more wide-reaching effects. It instilled in Southern slaves the possibility that emancipation was forthcoming, and they eventually equated emancipation with citizenship.

Butler had trouble gaining official action for coping with conditions at Fortress Monroe, but he fared better with the private sector. In New York, the American Missionary Association's representatives believed that citizenship for freed slaves was sure to result from the wars of finality. The missionaries had read daily about the situation and expressed heightened concerns for Butler's continuing dilemma when he was in Virginia because of the ever-swelling slave exodus corresponding with the government's lethargic legislative action. The American Missionary Association arrived soon in answer to Butler's call for help in addressing the needs of the growing tide of refugees.

Butler's ability to forge working relationships among military, political, and civil authorities was not unique to the Fortress Monroe situation. In fact, his success merely illustrates the talents he had long possessed. During civilian life, Butler had been a prominent, affluent Massachusetts criminal lawyer and politician. He was not only well known among the religious representatives with whom he worked closely, but later also became famous (or perhaps notorious, depending upon one's perspective) for his commands during the war.

In 1862, Butler left Virginia for reassignment in Louisiana, where the city of New Orleans soon knew him as Butler the "Beast" or "Brute. " Before General Butler left Louisiana in 1862, he had mustered two regiments of freedmen, known as Butler's Corps d'Afrique, with freedmen acting on their own behalf, even as commanding officers. Butler's political and legal acumen later helped the American Missionary Association (and therefore the Free Will Baptists among them) to establish the "Butler School" in Hampton, Virginia. When the American Missionary Association arrived to help Butler, among their number were many Free Will Baptists. "Fearing that the fugitives might be remanded to slavery," Lewis Tappan immediately dispatched Reverend Lewis C. Lockwood to the Virginia peninsula. The Baptists soon were there with Lockwood participating in the establishment of schools to educate the arriving freedmen.

When the North Carolina mission failed, the Free Will Baptists directed all their energies toward West Virginia. The new state, after all, was a crucial border state. They believed they could be more successful there because of the state's geographical proximity to the Northern expanse and the nation's capital. West Virginia had come to statehood in 1863, in order to thwart Virginia's political inequity, and end the historical contention between eastern and western Virginia. This helped the Baptists decide on Harpers Ferry as their mission center in the Shenandoah Valley. Harpers Ferry also offered a particular historical significance since it was the birthplace of John Brown's decisive action. His raid, after all, made the question of institutional slavery a matter of national conscience. His insurrection forced Americans to take sides on the issue of what "Life, Liberty, and the Pursuit of Happiness" would mean in the future of the nation.

Emancipation Oak photograph taken in 1907

"General Butler had settled all the perplexing questions in regard to them [slaves and later freedmen] by the happy application of the word 'contraband.'"

— *Louise Wood Brackett, 1892*

LOCKWOOD AND PEAKE'S MISSION SCHOOL

On September 15, 1861, Reverend Lewis Lockwood, under the auspices of the American Missionary Association, instituted a mission school in Hampton, Virginia, which was an antecedent to the Harpers Ferry Mission School and the direct ancestor of Hampton University.

Hampton had only recently been rid of its Confederate occupiers, and was by no means a safe haven for abolitionists and reformers. Along with the help and support from the Baptists, Lockwood also received unrelenting aid from Mary S. Peake. Prior to 1861, Peake, an educated mulatto, had been covertly teaching slave children to read, later giving some of her lessons under the famous "Emancipation Oak."

When the call arose, she capably assisted Lockwood's efforts to organize a school in one room of former President Tyler's home. Peake taught with Lockwood until she fell into a weakened, bedridden state from tuberculosis. Even then she met with scholars who visited her sickroom every day until her death, in February 1862, at thirty-nine. Despite her malady, Peake was responsible for operating the first officially endorsed mission school and also for establishing the basic educational standards—a combination of teaching, training, singing, and

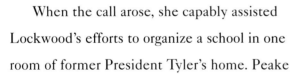

Plate from Mary S. Peake, the Colored Teacher at Fortress Monroe

religious schooling—by which mission teachers thereafter taught students. She had more than seventy students at one point, teaching some in the day and others at night. Lockwood was so impressed by Peake's unceasing devotion to education that he wrote a biography of her, entitled *Mary S. Peake, the Colored Teacher at Fortress Monroe.*

Hence, Butler's "property" dispute provided the door through which the American Mission Society stepped into Virginia to establish a mission school, which consequently influenced the missionary concentration throughout the region. Just one year later, in 1862, when it was thought safe, the American Missionary Association arrived en masse to relieve the plight of slaves. Free Will Baptists were among their number.

THE SEARCH FOR A MISSION BASE

Butler's response concerning slaves as "contraband" during the war made possible the institution of mission schools. Hard on the heels of the decision, the Free Will Baptist Home Mission Society readily began "fitting for freedom and Christian citizenship those for whom they had never forgotten to pray when they were in bondage." Before the war's end, the Home Mission Society selected Reverend Silas Curtis, one of its original founders, to develop a relief plan for freedmen and direct its implementation. Curtis was a natural choice. He was well known, respected, and possessed a reputation above reproach. He was also a meticulous Free Will Baptist officer, who had held many positions within the denominational infrastructure. He was, therefore, familiar with what it would take to implement a plan on the grand scale as visualized by the society. After the Fortress Monroe incident, the organization dispatched agents—Curtis among them—on fact-finding missions to Hampton, Virginia, and Beaufort, South Carolina. The intrepid Curtis "spent several weeks in South Carolina and Virginia as superintendent among the freedmen" as a representative of the mission's executive board.

During his fact-finding mission, Curtis visited schools, mission stations, teachers, and preachers in order to provide other members of the Home Mission Society's executive board with the information necessary to make future decisions. The Beaufort mission, however, disappointed the group. The failure of the mission in North Carolina by 1866 was due to Andrew Johnson's policies on Reconstruction. These returned properties to former Confederates in exchange for a pledge of loyalty to the Union. North Carolina was more than willing to embrace the president's policies given its recent past history. The state was equally opposed to external forces developing as potential obstructions to its autonomy.

When the Free Will Baptists enterprise in Beaufort finally failed, Curtis wrote Brackett—then located in Harpers Ferry—to advise, "I trust you will carefully, cautiously, & thoroughly look over the ground before you make a full decision about establishing a mission." Because the Freedmen's Bureau was directed to return properties to former Confederates, the deeper southern states much too unstable and the border areas seemed more viable to the founding denomination. After a short period, the Free Will Baptists decided on a more lucrative geographical location to establish mission schools with a higher education institution always in view. Although the mission in Beaufort was lost,

United States Christian Commission wagon train preparing to disembark during the war years.

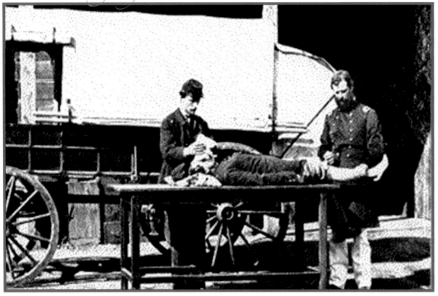

Field agents of the United States Sanitary Commission attend a wounded soldier.

Curtis remained generally optimistic, for he believed that "this was a grand opening for us [the society]—and I will do all in my power to have [the Shenandoah Valley] occupied by our teachers & missionaries." Curtis admitted his plan to Brackett: "I am anxious we should occupy all that district [in the Shenandoah Valley] those five towns—Harper's Ferry, Martinsburg, Shepherdstown, Charles Town & Berryville—those are historic places."

In 1865, the final arrangement between the Free Will Baptists and the American Missionary Association was committed to paper when "the articles of agreement between us [the Free Will Baptists] & the Am Miss Asson" entrusted the Shenandoah Valley to the Free Will Baptists for further missionary development.

At this time, Curtis was corresponding secretary and treasurer for the Free Will Baptist Home Mission Society. He used his position to begin recruiting teachers from Maine and Vermont for employment in the Shenandoah Valley. He was responsible not only for orienting new teachers to the society's expectations, but also for coordinating transportation and lodging for them on their journey south. Curtis wrote Brackett, stating that, if necessary, the Home Mission Society was prepared to transfer "two or four of [its] teachers now at Fortress Monroe" to the Shenandoah Mission until new Northern teachers could arrive, in order to begin immediately its work in the valley. The urgency evident in Curtis's letter indicates the depth of his desire to begin the mission of educating the freedmen.

The Shenandoah Mission

In 1865, through denominational collaboration, the Free Will Baptists conducted educational work among the freedmen

Philip Henry Sheridan,
Sheridan's Ride to the Front

throughout the Shenandoah Valley. They adapted quickly to assist with ongoing relief efforts to help care for the destitute, starving, and sickly former slaves, whose increasing numbers in the south created an emergency for government officials. It was, by any standard, a national crisis. Further, the slaves were not only suffering physically, but intellectually. At war's end, it is estimated that 90 to 95 percent of the freedmen were completely illiterate. How were freedmen to survive in a society whose forebears were the strongest proponents of education and even stronger examples of its value?

The Free Will Baptists were uniquely qualified to undertake such massive educational efforts. Years earlier, in 1862, the denomination dispatched several agents to assist in wartime relief programs in Virginia and North Carolina. After the war, they continued working to coordinate activities with the

Boston Educational Commission, American Missionary Association, National Freedmen's Relief Association, United States Christian Commission, and its partner, the Sanitary Commission, as well as the Freedmen's Bureau.

Much activity was centered on Harpers Ferry, since it was a natural gathering place for slaves. From the confluence of rivers there, freedmen could travel quickly in any cardinal direction through its natural gateway by water, by rail, or down the canal, although naturally freedmen

A Maryland Heights view of the Lockwood House (mission school and center) atop Camp Hill

were for the most part migrating northward. Since Harpers Ferry proved a natural safe haven toward which freedmen logically turned, it also seemed a good site upon which to build a school for freedmen. It had a hallowed place with reformers and freedmen alike, given its insurrectionist history. It was a natural place to commence the work of freeing former slaves from their intellectual bondage.

One of the men whose work would prove crucial to success at Harpers Ferry was Nathan Cook Brackett. Among the Free Will Baptists' most ardent reformists, Brackett during 1864-1865 served as an army chaplain and delegate to the United States Christian Commission attached to Major General Philip H. Sheridan.

As an army chaplain, Brackett had been uniquely positioned to assist in abolitionist efforts. Army chaplains working in the South specialized in helping deal with the "contraband"—that is, fugitive slaves. They assisted military personnel with "scattering fugitives [who] became a steady stream, which flowed faster than the armies marched." After completing a year's service in the army, principally in the Shenandoah Valley, Brackett visited other Free Will agents then working in South Carolina. Louise Wood Brackett claims that such a sojourn provided her husband with "a chance to compare this locality with others" over which the denomination deliberated, in order to determine the best location for its southern base of operations after the war officially ended.

When Brackett returned to Lewiston, Maine, in fall 1865, in time for the Free Will Baptist General Conference, the Home Mission Society was in fact convened with the General Conference in order to make a final decision regarding the mission's location. At this time, the Board of Directors persuaded Brackett to change his plans for South Carolina and embark instead on a mission in the Shenandoah Valley, which the Home Mission Society had finally decided upon as their field of operations.

THE MISSION SITE AT HARPERS FERRY

By 1865, Harper's Ferry, located in Jefferson County, West Virginia, had benefited from a rich, vigorous history. Before the onset of the Civil War, the township's population was not diverse. In fact, the population was then 90 percent white. This is despite the county's population of Native American inhabitants and the large number of farms in the largely agricultural community (463, according to the 1860 census), which likely required slave labor. The county had enjoyed a sustained period of prosperity. In combination with the end of the war, the county's increased agricultural growth—which also increased the demand for farm workers—helped spur a marked demographic shift.

When the Civil War ended, the population in Harpers Ferry was inexorably diversified. The town's inhabitants had been nearly equally represented in both the Confederate and Union armies during the war, but those who returned were joined by many freedmen and refugees seeking relief. By 1869, freedmen comprised 25 percent of the town's population. Perhaps at least a few had come to the region because of

John Brown's legacy, or to be closer to Washington, where slavery had been abolished. Consequently, in 1865, when the Free Will Baptists arrived to institute their network of mission schools, the town's population was racially diverse and had increased significantly.

This mixed population predicted racially mixed offspring. When the mission teachers arrived in Harpers Ferry by train just before Thanksgiving in 1865, mission teachers made several observations. The teachers began to clean the "dirty and dilapidated" Lockwood House where the school was to be housed, since they "found it in a bad condition, just as the soldiers had left it." As they did so, the mission teachers were surrounded by and "noticed with surprise that white children were present." Anne Dudley, one of the teachers, asked why they came, since Dudley and the other teachers were directed to organize classrooms and churches for freedmen and their children. The reply was: "'They are all niggers . . . Little Maggie Mason ha[s] a fair, white face, with straight, soft, brown hair; and merry Little Lee ha[s] blue eyes and flaxen hair, yet they had been slaves!"

The first site of the mission school at Harpers Ferry was the Lockwood House, which did not offer much in the way of creature comforts. After the war, the large imposing house had been abandoned. Its war-torn disfigurement was obvious when the teachers arrived in the cold, damp November weather. The town's winter seemed even colder than the temperature indicated because of the rivers' turbulence and its effect on the surrounding air. Two of the mission teachers, Anne Dudley and Sarah Jane Foster, took particular note of the "opening in the roof where a shell had unceremoniously entered" the rooftop, exposing the structure's interior to exterior elements. Brackett had been attached to Sheridan's roaming outfit as a Christian Commission delegate and was used to this type of makeshift bedlam. Anne Dudley remarked that Brackett "did not mind sleeping on the tent-ground, but the ladies were quite troubled about a resting-place, and finally decided, for very good reasons, to sleep on a table" instead.

"O yes, Miss Anne! I have cried myself to sleep many times thinking about being free, and I was glad I was born to die, for that was my only hope!"

—*Anne Dudley's report of a student's answer to the question, "Did you ever think about being free?"*

The Founding of Storer

THE FREEDMEN'S BUREAU

The Freedmen's Bureau acted as a significant player in the transition of governance from the Commonwealth of Virginia to the new state of West Virginia. In the arena of educational reform, the Bureau agents helped foster the beginnings of a Negro public school system during the administration of Governor Arthur I. Boreman. The Freedmen's Bureau was crucial for blacks in those parts of West Virginia where Confederate sympathy was still strong and where there was little support for the education of former slaves or other Negroes from public funds.

From the bureau's inception in 1865, Oliver Otis Howard, its chief administrator, had believed education to be the primary factor for elevating freedmen to a position of self-sufficiency and therefore social betterment. A report submitted to the bureau for June 1866 by R. Chandler, acting assistant commissioner, indicated that he was receiving information from seven schools scattered throughout the Shenandoah Valley, three in Virginia and four in West

General Oliver Otis Howard

Virginia (although the report itself makes no distinction between states). The Virginia schools were located in Massanutten, Front Royal, and Winchester. The Massanutten school was organized by the American Missionary Association. In June 1866, its head teacher, G. H. Hammond, was directly responsible for thirty-five students, although his official enrollment listed forty-five. Farther down the valley, the Front Royal and Winchester schools averaged forty and 115 students, respectively. The Front Royal school, under the leadership of Lincoln Given, also had been organized by the Free Will Baptists, while the Winchester school, under the supervision of R. J. Young, was instituted by the Presbyterian Church of Pittsburgh. In the Lower Shenandoah Valley, the Free Will Baptists organized schools in Harpers Ferry, Charles Town, Shepherdstown, and Martinsburg.

Thus, in June 1866, the Free Will Baptists were responsible for managing five of seven schools then in operation in the Lower Shenandoah Valley, and for educating 234 students, over 60 percent of the freedmen enrolled. During the first postwar year, as its agents actively worked to collaborate with Northern philanthropic representatives, the bureau claimed that in the South it was involved in the establishment of 4,239 schools employing 9,307 teachers and serving 247,333 students. Mission teachers working during the 1866 school term in the Shenandoah Valley were Smith and Libby (Charles Town), Wright (Shepherdstown), Libby and Foster (Harpers Ferry), and Dudley (Martinsburg). These teachers were in high demand, forcing at least one of their number—Libby—to travel between the Charles Town and Harpers Ferry schools.

THE MISSION TEACHERS AT HARPERS FERRY

Teaching in missionary schools was a demanding task. It begs the question: What were the young women like who made a commitment to the mission schools? The New England mission teachers commissioned to Southern states were dependable, moral, and adaptable. Locating and recruiting young teachers with these characteristics proved to be crucial to the venture. Even the journey south to arrive at the postings was strenuous, difficult, and time-consuming, often involving an arduous three-day journey. Silas Curtis and George Whipple, the corresponding secretary for the American Missionary Association, coordinated travel arrangements for teachers. New York was the halfway marker for most of Curtis's teachers on their journey, many of whom were recruited from various northeastern townships. Curtis and Whipple became expert at making travel arrangements. They collaborated with sympathetic commanders, ship's captains, train conductors, carriage drivers, administrative personnel, ticketing agents, and other like-minded individuals to create a reliable transportation

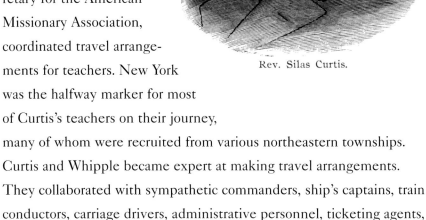

Rev. Silas Curtis.

network routing teachers into the South. These various individuals were persuaded—more often than not willingly—to aid the missionary societies.

The first teachers had to be strong and determined. In order to reach their mission assignments, teachers prepared for a trip that could involve four or five different connections from different locations. The first leg of the journey south entailed leaving home, many for the first time. Influenced by the Victorian era in which they lived, however, such women were immured to self-sacrifice—or perhaps they viewed the experience as a chance to escape many societal constraints. In either case, by committing to work with Southern freedmen in situations that were at times hostile, the teachers recruited by the Home Mission Society exhibited a powerful sense of self-sacrifice in order to achieve general social betterment. The work they were about to encounter was physically and emotionally demanding. The teachers endured the trip, and the great majority proved themselves to be hardy and even adventurous travelers, they were more than ready for their postings.

Before the missionary teachers made the long trek, the teachers-to-be agreed to meet with their colleagues at a central location for final preparations. There were two possible rendezvous points for proximity and congenial accommodations: Concord, New Hampshire (Curtis's location), or Lewiston, Maine. It is probable that most of the teachers met at Concord, since Curtis, as the Home Mission Society's official corresponding secretary, was responsible for contacting and directing them. Curtis had the new teachers sign a "circular," which detailed the society's expectations and terms of agreement for employment. Since Curtis took his duties and responsibilities seriously, the teachers most likely were encouraged to meet at his office in Concord, where his oversight would be guaranteed.

The second rendezvous site was Lewiston, Maine, the home of Bates College, formerly the Maine State Seminary, which was chartered on March 16, 1855, as "the chief educational institution of the Free Baptists in New England." Several mission teachers in fact were trained in the seminary's programs. From Lewiston, the teachers then traveled southeast to Portland, a thirty-five-mile trip in order to reach the coastal city's harbor. They sailed from Portland down the Atlantic coastline to New York harbor and from there into the Chesapeake Bay, finally arriving at Baltimore, Maryland. From Baltimore, teachers took a car on the Baltimore & Ohio Railroad to reach their field commissions. The Shenandoah Mission teachers, as per Curtis's instructions, took the mountainous western spur of the Baltimore & Ohio Railroad, heading for Harpers Ferry, where they first met Brackett, who would become their direct supervisor.

Additionally, the mission teachers had to be willing to extend their level of self-sacrifice to their own remuneration. In 1864, the Free Will Baptist Home Mission Society paid teachers $10 per month. This was consistent with the earlier salary standard set by the American Missionary Association. The society, in 1865, however conferred with other societies on the matter of "fixed uniform salaries" for mission teachers. In Silas Curtis's terms, "we agreed to allow all $15.00 per month & pay traveling expenses and board; & then give all who are able and willing to make any reduction, the privilege & what ever they say they will give monthly for the mission will be deducted monthly and credited to them in the receipts of the 'Star'." Several teachers

reverted $2 to $3 dollars per month to further demonstrate a degree of financial commitment to the mission effort, for which they were duly recognized in the *Morning Star*.

Last, but most assuredly not least, the Shenandoah Mission's teachers tended to be well educated. Philanthropic societies like the Free Will Baptist Home Mission Society conscientiously tried to maintain high standards among those sent to educate freed slaves. Many graduated from New England colleges and were driven by altruistic motives. Mission teachers thus were devoted to schooling freedmen in much the same manner and with the same methods by which they themselves had been educated in New England. In fact, it can be argued that they adopted the design of Northern institutions in the South. Anne Dudley, for example, graduated in 1864 from the Maine State Seminary. In the same year Nathan Wood Brackett graduated from Dartmouth. Sarah Foster was "a teacher by training," although not by college degree, having worked in various educational settings in Maine before arriving in Harpers Ferry. Wright and Gibbs, according to denominational correspondence, were experienced teachers willing to accept a new challenge in the South. The model for higher education that the young teachers had experienced, therefore, seems to have been more an academic rather than proselytizing one, although the religious content of the classrooms where they taught remains clear.

SOUTHERN RULES AND PRECONCEPTIONS: TWO TEACHERS' VOICES

Among the first teachers to arrive at Harpers Ferry in 1865 were Anne S. Dudley and Sara Jane Foster. From Dudley's reports and Foster's diary entries made between 1865 and 1867, a multidimensional perspective on what life was like for the early mission teachers who came to teach freedmen in the Lower Shenandoah Valley emerges.

During Anne Dudley's first seventeen months in West Virginia, she was frequently moved from one school to another. The teacher was in Harpers Ferry for one month, and then she was dispatched by Brackett to go to Charles Town, in the same county. During her stay in Charles Town, Anne Dudley established the Charles Town Mission School. She taught freedmen there for four months, but was then later moved to Martinsburg, where she stayed an entire year. During this year in Martinsburg, the educator taught 115 students in night school and 515 in day and night schools combined. Her enrollment for Sabbath schools was 320. She visited over 700 colored families, distributed fifty Bibles, and issued sixty-one other types of books, so that students— adults and children alike—could practice reading skills.

Collectively, Anne Dudley's students received from her 11,972 pages of various religious tracts on subjects ranging from conversion to temperance, and Sunday School papers with accounts of biblical figures. With such vigorous activity, Dudley became familiar not only with her students, but also with the response of local populations to her ongoing efforts.

Anne Dudley was an idealist, but not naive. She harbored few illusions about the reception that she would receive outside of her classroom. She came with no great expectations of general social acceptance, and she found this preconception to be accurate, at least in the beginning. There were many stubborn adherents to the failed Southern cause, and prejudices against people of color were deeply ingrained among some segments of the population. From the first, her status was precarious, to say the least. When Nathan Wood Brackett first sent Dudley to Charles Town around New Year's in 1866 to institute a mission school for that township, she traveled under military escort due to ongoing tension in the region.

Her caution was well founded. She soon reported to the Free Will Baptists-Home Mission Society that "I could get no permanent boarding place for nearly two months (for it would have been a lifelong disgrace for a Virginian to board Yankee teachers, and the Rubicon once passed, there could be no return to friends and society, no more than over the walls of caste in India, as public sentiment was

"I have no hope that the great mass of the present generation of southern people will ever be friends to the freedmen or northern people. I believe they would put a yoke on every neck, and a lash on every back that would not bow down to the god of slavery, or annihilate us as quick today as when they first fired on Fort Sumter!"

—*Anne Dudley in an 1867 report to the Home Missionary Society* then) so I was there alone, boarding myself and teaching day and night, until I had 150 scholars of all ages and complexions," teaching the rudiments of reading to all "from white to black, and of all ages, from four to fifty-five years."

After Dudley recognized the level of preconceptions and stigma attached to "complexions." The Maine-trained teacher also reported that "the blackest child in the school is one of the best scholars I ever saw. They certainly make wonderful progress under the circumstances." Dudley may have been resented by many outside her school, but the teacher found that her long hours in the classroom were much appreciated by the freedmen residing there in the valley.

Despite social proscription, many hardships, and long hours, Dudley's relationship with the freedmen, and therefore their community, ultimately must have been quite rewarding and inspiring. When the freedmen learned to pray in the manner of tutored schoolchildren, their first prayers were filled with requests to the "Almighty God for protection of their teachers."

Dudley reported to the *Morning Star* that "all the colored people manifested the greatest kindness towards us. I shall never forget the oft repeated prayer: 'O Lord, bless de teacher dat come a far distance to teach us. Front and fight her battles, and bring her safe home to Glory, if you please, Massa Jesus!'"

Dudley was not the only mission teacher to record her students' prayers. Sarah Jane Foster recorded in her diary that the former slaves "all seem to know us as if by intuition and welcome us very warmly, but always with due respect," indicated by the way in which the students prayed for them. Foster later recalled the degree of genuineness and heartfelt concern offered through her students' prayers. While at a meeting in Harpers Ferry, she recollected that "the prayer of one woman was unequaled for its simple child-like confidence, appropriateness, and a certain touching poetic beauty that words would fail to reproduce."

The prayers offered by the students likely served to reinvigorate the teachers and renewed their sense of purpose and mission as they tirelessly traversed from school to school teaching, singing, and preaching the Gospel. Perhaps this is why the teachers also recorded the occasional conversion experiences of students.

> *"She would say,—* 'Dear Father didn't you promise?' or 'didn't you say, so and so?' with the most perfect freedom of address and each petition ended in a sort of chanted rhythmical 'Jesus if it be thy will.'"
>
> One petition I will try to quote. It was this,— 'Dear Father we had good reasons to know that you's been quartered here at Harper's Ferry, an, now we wants you to come again, Jesus if it be thy will, an, please don't ride, way off roun, but jist come right here an take a gentle ride roun, amongst us, Jesus if it be they will.'"
>
> —*Sarah Jane Foster,* *recording an adult student's prayer in her diary, 1867*

Shortly after Dudley was transferred to Martinsburg, she established a Free Will Baptist church on Raleigh Street. Dudley's first convert there was a woman known as Jennie. Anne Dudley grew very fond of her. After Jennie's absence for a period, Dudley said, "I missed her for a long time." When Dudley finally had the time to go searching for Jennie, she "found her and her child at last, in a miserable hovel, sick and helpless." Jennie told Dudley that "when she could work no longer she was thrown into the street, and lay nearly all day in the burning hot sun, when this colored family found her and took her in." Dudley sadly reported that "the next time [she] saw Jennie she was in her coffin, wrapped in that sweet sleep, 'from which none ever wake to weep,' and I doubt not her happy spirit is in heaven."

Alcohol abuse seemed to be a fairly common problem among adult students. Anne Dudley often warned one of these students of the wicked ends and evils of alcohol. According to an address she gave to the Free Will Baptists-Home Mission Society, she vividly recalled that one day the man appeared at her schoolroom door and proclaimed: "'O Miss Anne! I have come to tell you I have found Jesus! You told me true, —I was very wicked. I wanted to come and ask you to pray for me, but I was afraid. I went over the hills among the rocks and prayed many times—at last it was all light—now I am so happy. O Miss Anne I don't want any more whiskey—I don't think of it!'"

Dudley reported that she "could only listen in tears" when the man described his life of sin and subsequent conversion. Thereafter, in the same speech, she said the man was decidedly in tune with the Spirit, claiming that "I wish you [here in Dover, New Hampshire] could hear him singing his favorite tune, 'I hear de heaben bells ringin.'"

After this, Dudley added that "no white minister in the city [of Martinsburg] has ever come into our meetings, and only an occasional visit from a colored one has cheered us on our way, but the good shepherd over all has led us through green pastures and by still waters; shut the mouths of lions; made the sword powerless, and brought us on our way singing victory."

"The chivalrous students of the Military Institute of Lexington have caused our teachers much trouble. One night a party of them went and demanded one of the scholars, saying, they were going to shoot him. When the teachers could not persuade them to go away, and the rowdies were getting desperate, Miss Harper, one of the teachers, stepped forward and told them if they shot Ben they would shoot her first, and with wonderful courage drove them away, and had them arrested and taken to court. The matter was hushed up, and Gen. Lee sent a note of apology to the teachers."

—*Anne Dudley, 1867*

But Dudley was ultimately confronted with a particularly trouble-some incident that was stricken from the official public record. She said that she had been in Martinsburg, Berkeley County, for slightly "more than a year" after leaving Charles Town, in Jefferson County. At this time, between 1866 and 1867, Dudley and the teachers at the Martinsburg Mission School began to be visited frequently by the cadets on furlough from the Virginia Military Institute in Lexington. Dudley recounted that a group of rowdy cadets demanded that a student named Ben be handed over to them so that they could shoot him. The bravery of one of the teachers, a Miss Harper, saved the day. She claimed the cadets would have to shoot her first before they took Ben. She proceeded then to drive them away and even had the unruly bunch arrested. This seems to have been hushed up, and ended with a written apology from General Lee.

Mrs. Anne S. Dudley Bates.

Not unlike the event with the cadets from Lexington, there were other discouraging incidents intended to impede the teachers from pro-ceeding with their mission to educate freedmen. "Some rascals broke down our door about nine" tonight, Foster wrote. Foster's boarding chaperone, Mr. Hoke, "advised [her] to stay away from [the] school" building after she was seen walking in public down Queen Street with Mr. Hopewell," a colored supporter of the school. Foster admitted that she "walked through the street all the way with Mr. Hopewell, just to show that [she] did not mean to be driven off by the roughs."

On Thursday, January 25, 1866, Foster recorded that "our meeting was disturbed and some of the Colored people fired a pistol after the intruders, and gave chase and caught two. They have the names of two more. Capt. McKenzie was sent for and took them to jail. " These kinds of incidents were a chronic problem for several years.

At the beginning of her assignment in Martinsburg, however, Foster's naivete, in contrast to Anne Dudley's more pessimistic out-look, caused her to make quite a different observation about the town—at least initially. When she arrived there, she observed "this place is intensely Union. A rebel is worse off here than farther North . . . .The town here has suffered much, as have all places in the vicinity. I can but own that our army practiced more vandalism than was neces-sary or excusable." Foster eventually changed her opinion.

On December 16, 1865, almost three weeks after her initially positive observation, Foster wrote a much different description of local conditions in her diary. "The 'New Era,' an opposition paper here, week before last contained a slight fling at us and our work . . . I sometimes hear myself pointed out as a 'nigger teacher,' and people, especially children, stare in on passing the school-room, but we are as yet entirely undisturbed, and likely to remain so." A by-product of the recent war was "social proscrip-tion," which was specifically directed toward white teachers from the North working in the South with black students. Dudley noted the "sting of contempt and scorn as we feel it poured on us who go at the bidding of our Divine Master to teach the poor and needy." Foster seemingly did not fully comprehend the broad spectrum of proscription.

Truly innocent of the highly circumscribed conduct toward racial relations commonly understood among people reared in the South, Foster caused a great stir when she failed to adhere to local norms of behavior. A social boundary, unspoken but very real, was observed regarding public interaction between the races. The strongest taboos of all were against the mixing of white females and black males in any social, private, or public context. It was an unspoken social more in the South that both races understood without question.

When Foster, accompanied by Mr. Hopewell, one of her adult students, was observed walking down Queen Street in Martinsburg, the Hoke family, with whom Foster was boarding, became "really alarmed." They feared, with good cause, that a mob might form. Captain J. H. McKenzie, an assistant superintendent of the Freedmen's Bureau who was assigned to Martinsburg, shared these fears. The captain retrieved his pistol when he sensed existing tensions had been compounded by Foster's transgression, and an escalation of the stakes might result. With his pistol at his side, McKenzie escorted Foster from the schoolroom under guard. The young teacher's subsequent response was genuine, but it was one that the nineteenth-century Southern society was unprepared to accept. "I shall treat all well who treat me well, both black and white," Foster declared.

In effect, Foster was practicing what she had learned during her own Sunday School training in Gray, Maine, a principle that articulated her own heartfelt rendition of the Golden Rule. Nonetheless, her "indiscretion" proved disconcerting to a society already nervous about the changes occurring within its traditional social norms. Her altruism was genuine, but her judgment in this instance is, perhaps more questionable. Still one may speculate whether this defiant act gave courage to others whose consciences were troubled by injustice, but who bowed under the heavy weight of long-standing custom.

From Foster we also gain some insight into the mission teachers' relationships with the families who hosted them. When Nathan Wood Brackett received teachers at the Shenandoah Mission, it was his duty to locate sympathetic families with whom they could board once outlying mission schools became operational. These families, on whom benevolent societies heavily relied, were often locally prominent and held high ethical standards for themselves and the societies in which they lived. They believed that the nation's postwar Reconstruction—and therefore social betterment for freedmen—depended on shared responsibilities to rectify the iniquitous actions of the past. Brackett, a resourceful person, was able to locate several of these sympathetic—and brave—families.

In 1865, when Foster and Wright were organizing the mission school in Martinsburg, the former wrote about her benevolent sponsors. Foster boarded with the Hoke family at 201 Martin Street in Martinsburg, a convenient address, since the residence put Foster well within relatively safe walking distance of her school. Foster clearly held her host family in high regard, and her respect and admiration for the Hokes seems quite deep. In her diary she wrote, "We are boarding with a most excellent Union family named Hoke. I give the name because their devoted loyalty throughout our great struggle for right, is worthy of a more enduring record than I can give. I never weary of hearing them tell of the varied scenes of the past four years. It seems strange to realize that I am where war was so long a dread and actual presence, and I am sure that those who were all the while faithful, merit immortality, if earthly fame can bestow it."

The position of trust and authority that the teachers held among their students helped to foster a great sense of responsibility in the instructors. These teachers, Dudley and Foster included, came to care not just for the educational needs of the children they tended, but also for their physical well-being. In the first year, with the coldest part of the 1865 winter yet ahead, Dudley and the other teachers expressed a growing concern for the students' health, pleas that prompted Curtis to promise additional warm clothing.

In the process of distributing such articles of clothing to their students, the teachers made regular home visitations. Sometimes, though, on particularly cold days, the school itself provided shelter for the impoverished students. On January 7, 1866, for example, Sarah Jane Foster realized that it was "a terribly cold day" and "it was too cold to send the children home." Water was freezing in her schoolroom, while the streets and walkways were icy. Comparing her home state of Maine to West Virginia, Foster claims, "I have felt this cold snap as bad as I ever felt the cold in New England."

On another occasion, Foster claimed that "several of the little ones were so cold on those cold mornings that I had to take their hands in mine to warm them before they could bear to approach the fire." Often mission teachers designated a fire-tender to fuel, stock, kindle, and start fires in schoolrooms early in the morning before

students arrived. The annual cold snap during the month of January must have stimulated Foster to locate an effective fire-tender. "I have at last made out to get my fire into good hands, and now have a warm room mornings," Foster wrote with enthusiasm, on January 9, in her diary.

EARLY STUDENTS

Despite the often-inclement weather, students in the early days flocked to the school. Foster admiringly noted that "some of them come long distances . . . . I wonder that they come at all in this cold weather." A few of Foster's students traveled the distance because they were voracious learners. For this group, their eagerness to succeed and capacity for learning seemingly could not be sated. One such student was the ironically—or appropriately— named John Brown, whose performance was stellar.

In her diary, Foster indicates that "Mr. Brackett had been urging [John Brown] to go to Lewiston, Maine to school" in order to continue his education in branches higher than could be offered at the time in West Virginia.

Anne Dudley also recorded some of the progress of one of her gifted students. Two years after Dudley had been teaching in the Shenandoah Valley, she traveled to New England for the Baptist Convention. While there, Dudley found that several of the churchmen and women retained various preconceptions and misconceptions about her work. The expectations of Dudley's Northern colleagues for educating the people served by the Shenandoah Valley missions were apparently rather low. Dudley was likely to describe her more exceptional students enrolled in the mission schools. Some not only demonstrated high intellectual ability, but they—perhaps more importantly—demonstrated that they were attuned to the political climate surrounding them. In 1867, in order to demonstrate to the Home Mission Society the intelligence exhibited by her students in the South, Dudley submitted the following poem as evidence of their abilities, in which Lincoln and Johnson figure:

> "'Eight years ago, when I was ruled,
> Did I ever think I would sit in School?
> But President Lincoln—God bless his name—
> Through him, my labor is not in vain.
> He did his best, and left the rest,
> For Johnson to guide the poor oppressed,
> Now I am free, and shall always be,
> As long as the north and south can agree,
> And then before I'll be a slave,
> I'll be carried to my grave!'"

Although it is apparent that Dudley's student was black, all other details remain unknown. The essential conception conveyed by the work, however, is that the student possessed the ability to exploit the creative possibilities of poetic language and structure, had a true political consciousness, and was effective at the expression of the social climate of the era.

The measurable impact of the missions was greatly encouraging to the Free Will Baptist-Home Mission Society, and the gratitude of those served by the missionaries was heartfelt. Therefore the Free Will Baptists proceeded with a plan to found a college. To accomplish this, they enlisted the financial support and political sagacity of several denominational men, one Maine philanthropist, and several key politicians. They all were moved to this act of conscience in order to share the responsibility for reconstructing the Union, and educating the nation's freedmen.

STORER COLLEGE TAKES FORM

The school that eventually became Storer College would not have been possible without the tireless efforts and forward thinking of a small but dedicated group of Free Will Baptist men. Oren Cheney, Silas Curtis, Alexander Hatch Morrell, and Nathan Cook Brackett ultimately became responsible for shouldering the effort that brought the school to fruition—of creating the governing commissions, raising matching funds, and hiring appropriate staff. Although in the history of Storer, the names of these four men stand out, their work was supported by and indeed would have been impossible without individual and collective efforts of fellow crusaders: Ebenezer Knowlton, George Tiffany Day, Jonathan Brewster, and Isaac Dalton Stewart, among many others.

Likewise, John Storer's initial pledge of seed money for the institution proved crucial, and Senator William Pitt Fessenden and Representative James A. Garfield lent their support from Washington. These emancipationists, college presidents, congressmen, politicians, denominational officers, soldiers, legislators, editors, federal emissaries, judges, ministers, and principled men comprised the "Commission for the Promotion of Education in the South."

The Founding of Storer

THE PROCESS BEGINS: The Commission for the Promotion of Education in the South

In addition to acquiring use of the property at Harpers Ferry, Oren Cheney and his fellow workers had to get down to the business of actually planning their school. In 1867, they began by forming what they called a "body politic." This unit was created to oversee the organization of the school and also to direct John Storer's beneficence by both establishing a permanent school for freedmen and instituting a home mission center in support of the school. By locating their mission center close to the school, the commissioners believed the denomination could better direct Storer's endowment, regulate the school, supervise teachers, and retrieve important information that would help shape the school's overall development. On June 6, 1867, in Northwood, New Hampshire, four months after Cheney's initial meeting with John Storer in Sanford, the Commission for the Promotion of Education in the South was organized.

The commission was organized by, and composed of men, who believed that by investing in social betterment through the education of former slaves, they were indeed improving the quality of living for all American citizens. The scope of this belief—the common betterment of all—is directly attributable to the Free Will Baptists' spiritual father, Benjamin Randal, whose sense of "universal" application made the founding not only of the denomination but also of Storer College possible. The commission's activities as a "body politic" must be understood from the denomination's theological framework, out of which the group worked to institute a Southern college. The

commission's act of conscience served as a direct demonstration of its faith. Why it was such a demonstration, and how it was that this led to the foundation of the college, are essential components for understanding the genesis of Storer College.

AN ACT OF CONSCIENCE

During the eighteenth and nineteenth centuries, as the Free Will Baptists began to evolve and grow, they were known for their willingness to challenge prevailing attitudes in order to help others. After the Civil War, they believed they were responsible for sharing in the Reconstruction of the South. By doing so, they were not only improving the lives of the people who had lived there, but they were also improving the places in which those people had lived. It is with this intent that the Free Will Baptists surged into the South to improve social conditions, and educate former slaves, freedmen, war refugees, and public indigents "without distinction of race or color."

The two-word phrase "without distinction" was an important aspect of Free Will Baptist ideo-theology. "Without distinction"—a simple phrase—appeared throughout the denomination's correspondences, and it then routinely appeared in college catalogues while the school was in operation. The inclusion of these words indicated that the Baptists were prepared to make no exceptions against, or to make no preconceptions about, any student seeking an education. Therefore, the ideology behind enslavement or segregation solely based on race was simply not acceptable. It was this same phrase that, in 1867, gave rise to a "fierce debate" among members of the West

Virginia Legislature when the "Commission for the Promotion of Education in the South" made application for a school charter in Wheeling. Baptist beliefs regarding "choice" and, most particularly, "free will" were integral characteristics of their faith. To their way of thinking, individuals made conscious choices based on their free will to do so. "Free will" and "choice" evolved as the primary religious and moral antecedents for the Baptists' work to institute schools in the South by the war's end.

CHOICE AND FREE WILL

Choice, and therefore the exercise of free will, were the essential theological distinctions that set the Free Will Baptist denomination apart from Calvinist ideas about the omniscient, omnipotent power of God. John Calvin believed that an all-powerful, all-knowing God required the divine foreknowledge of those to be saved—the elect—and those doomed to hell—the damned. Benjamin Randal differed greatly with John Calvin's theological position, modeling his beliefs after Jan Armenius, the Dutch reformer. A godly predisposition, according to Calvin's proposition, assures salvation for some while not for others. According to Benjamin Randal's point of view, however, the doctrine of predestination drew into question the whole of Christianity. Why then the artificial cycle of penitence, confession, atonement, redemption, and salvation, if individual fates have been predetermined? Consequently, Randal, a product of the eighteenth century's "Great Awakening," viewed Calvinist theology "as being unduly harsh as well as being an affront to common sense in that [it] tended to undermine all morality. . . ."

Randal saw in Christianity a message of simple faith guided by choice. Those who adhered to the denomination's religious canon during the years of the terrible struggle between North and South thus deeply believed that at the war's end, the choices they made as individuals had consequences for the many. Their "universal" perspective, their conviction that they were making the correct decision to institute a school in the south for the personal and public betterment, was indeed a principle founded in their faith. The Free Will Baptists therefore proceeded with their plan to educate former slaves guided by their belief and convictions. Their mission schools' success and very survival in the post–Civil War Shenandoah Valley hinged on their faith in God, each other, and their fellow men.

The Founding of Storer

OREN B. CHENEY, EMANCIPATIONIST FROM BIRTH

Oren Burbank Cheney whose father, Moses, "held an unpopular position of conductor on the Underground Railroad and helped flying fugitives on their way to liberty" was born December 10, 1816, into a stolidly abolitionist family, a fact that predisposed him to decry slavery from an early age. His family was a part of a social milieu steeped in fervent social activism. Cheney's memories, recounted in diary entries, include reminiscences about frequent visits to the family home from long-standing abolitionists and activist ex-slaves alike. Frederick Douglass, Harriet Livermore, and Nathaniel Peabody Rogers, among others, came to call at the Cheney home. Their visits often corresponded with stops on the lecture circuit as they traveled to speak at antislavery meetings.

Cheney's involvement with the abolitionist cause grew even more determined as the country inexorably progressed toward war. When Fort Sumter was fired upon, Cheney was moved to write in his diary

"the freemen of the north are ready. Slavery must die. I am ready to die for freedom."

His activities over the next several months give clear evidence of this resolve. Cheney's wife, Emeline Burlingame-Cheney, wrote that her husband grew increasingly concerned about the national situation and its consequences. After the skirmish at Fort Sumter, on April 12,

Administrative offices of the United States Christian Commission in Washington, D.C. (c.1861)

1861, she noted, "Mr. Cheney could not keep away from 'the front.'" In 1861, he began a routine of traveling to Washington, D.C., and surrounding vicinities during the summer months to work with the United States Christian Commission. Cheney wrote in his diary that he "visited

Camp Jackson . . .[where] thousands of soldiers came into Washington" on a regular basis.

Quite clearly, the sights of the nation at war overcame Cheney. "His country's cause, especially that of the freedom of the slaves, lay so close to his heart," Mrs. Cheney wrote, "that his newspaper articles [in the *Morning Star*] and diary were full of the passing events" of the day. A devout Free Will Baptist, Cheney believed that the abolitionist fervor of his denomination could not help but influence those in charge of the war.

Ultimately, it was in his religion that Cheney saw what he believed was the true path to freedom for slaves. From the beginning of his involvement with the abolitionist movement, he firmly believed that the education of freedmen was the first step toward their true emancipation. Cheney arranged a meeting and conferred with the editor of the *Morning Star*, as to the desirability of sending "to the President a Free Baptist memorial, officially signed, asking for immediate emancipation." This conference with his fellow Baptists indicates that the congregation was promoting "immediate emancipation" and that Cheney was determined to pursue his goals, even as far as the White House and the Office of the President.

After the war, one of Cheney's primary goals was the establishment of an educational institution. On the morning of April 17, 1867, Cheney

Rev. O. B. Cheney, D. D.

US secretary and Senator William P. Fessenden visited Secretary Edwin M. Stanton, United States secretary of war, to discuss abandoned government properties in Harpers Ferry, then under jurisdiction of the War Department. Unfortunately, Secretary Stanton was "in Ohio-returns," (meaning that the election results were not yet finalized) and he was therefore unavailable to Cheney and Fessenden. Undaunted, Cheney wrote to Nathan Cook Brackett, stating, "it is my duty to remain here until I see him [Stanton]; and I propose to do so."

Any future communication with Cheney by Brackett was to be addressed "care of W. Hamlin Esq. Office of the Secretary of the Senate."

Cheney's efforts went even further. After speaking to General Oliver Otis Howard, who had "applied to President Sears for a donation from the Peabody fund for his college [Howard University]," Cheney notes his determination to "follow suit in reference to ours." On April 17, 1867, Cheney did just that—diligently appealed for help from administrators in Washington in order to obtain properties in Harpers Ferry.

At some point in this journey, Cheney developed a "new idea" for the denominational school, which he shared with Brackett in a letter dated April 17, 1867. In his letter, Cheney suggested to Brackett "that if we can get the lease of the 25 acres and the buildings thereon for a term of years, then we strike for the purchase of the whole government property at the Ferry. We can purchase the property probably at a lower price than any other party, for we want it for the public good—and if we can get possession of it, we can sell it and make a good profit by way of endowing the college. I hope you will not let the business matters at the Ferry be delayed a day. If matters work well here, you must close a bargain at almost any price."

CHENEY AND JOHN STORER

In early February 1867, Oren Cheney, the president of Bates College, traveled approximately sixty miles from his campus just outside Lewiston, Maine, to visit John Storer in Sanford. The visit was more than a meeting of friends—its greater purpose was to enlist Storer's financial assistance in support of education. When Cheney arrived in Sanford, he discovered that Storer was preparing to "execute a plan." Storer intended to bequeath $10,000 to an

"organized body" having the capacity to establish a school for freedmen—an institution that potentially could evolve into a "permanent blessing to the colored race" in the South.

After a long, introspective conversation that did not end until midnight, Storer finally confessed to Cheney that "'I should like to give it [the bequest] to your people [Free Will Baptists] for I honor them for the position they have taken'" against slavery. During this extended discussion, Storer eventually had committed $10,000 to the Free Will Baptists, contingent upon rigid requirements. These conditions were that the denomination organize a committee, raise matching funds, manage both the school and its endowment, and locate the school in a permanent facility with potential growth in mind—all before January 1, 1868. To even the most casual observer, the task for the small denomination might have appeared overwhelming. Nonetheless, on February 6, 1867, Storer and Cheney "wrote out a plan for a Freedmen's College" in the South that was endorsed by both men.

JOHN STORER, BENEFACTOR AND PHILANTHROPIST

John Storer was born on January 18, 1796, in the southeastern coastal town of Wells, Maine. When he was fourteen, he left his family to attend Bowdoin College, from which he graduated in 1812.

By 1820, at the age of twenty-four, Storer had married Meribah Hobbs, with whom he would have six children. He was working as a shipping clerk in Kennebunk for Benjamin Smith and Horace Porter when his employers suggested that lucrative business opportunities in shipping trades were possible for him in nearby Sanford.

The Maine District had just shed its northern Massachusetts territory status when, on March 15, 1820, it was awarded its statehood in conjunction with the Missouri Compromise. This primed the area for a business boom, particularly along the intercoastal waterways and rivers. Sanford was situated along the Mousam River in the southwestern portion of Maine in York County, bordering New Hampshire. If Storer was willing to relocate there, Smith and Porter offered to financially underwrite a new business enterprise. This is how John Storer ended up in the river town of Sanford at a time when the potential for capitalist ventures was rising and the question of slavery was growing.

In fact, New England as a whole was the center of antislavery sentiment, particularly among religious organizations. While conducting business between Sanford and Portland, Storer likely came in contact with several New England Baptists, Congregationalists, Unitarians, and Transcendentalists. Many of these people were antislavery advocates who had organized various aspects of their denomination's opposition to slavery in the New England states. Although Storer was a professed Congregationalist, he frequented the company of Free Will Baptists because he "was deeply interested in the history and aims of [the]

denomination" during his lifetime. It seems that the energetic businessman admired the social activism of the denomination. Storer first became aware of the Baptists' wide-ranging activities through his housekeeper, Mary Bachelder, who was a devout Free Baptist and often read to her employer from such Baptist publications as the Freewill Baptist Register, the *Morning Star*, and the *Freewill Baptist Magazine* or *Quarterly*. Although his health was not always good, Storer was still mentally and socially adept. He was a keen businessman, and he used every opportunity to keep abreast of prominent social issues of his day.

Bachelder's reading sessions kept Storer informed on the issues dear to activists and reformers in the mid-nineteenth century. Temperance, women's suffrage, antislavery, emancipation, benevolent and missionary enterprises, colonization, and territorial expansion (such as the corresponding actions out of which Maine's statehood was acquired) were targets for these writings. So outspoken on these issues was the Baptist journal, the *Morning Star*, that it drew the attention of New Hampshire legislators, who brought a "cruel pressure . . . against [it] on account of its outspoken position concerning slavery." For a time, the presses of the Free Will Baptist Printing Establishment were stopped due to its controversial editorial positions. From such radical efforts, Storer received a solid education on humanitarian goals as conceived by the most far-reaching reformers. So concerned was he about the plight of the slaves that he traveled directly to Harpers Ferry to speak with Brackett, "who was then organizing and superintending mission schools in the Valley of Virginia."

The Founding of Storer

During these years, Storer witnessed the unswerving dedication of the small Baptist denomination as it played out through the great events of his lifetime. Probably one of the last letters he wrote to the denomination before his death, dated October 3, 1867, best describes his sentiment toward them. In this missive, he claims, "'I knew your people more than sixty years ago, and have traced their progress with wonder and admiration since; and can but exclaim, 'What hath God wrought!'" This level of commitment to the denomination and their history ultimately led Storer to proclaim to Cheney during their 1867 winter meeting that because of "the position they had taken" against slavery he viewed the Free Will Baptists with "honor" for their strong sense of human dignity.

Unfortunately, Storer was never able to make the long journey to witness firsthand the operation of the "Southern enterprise" that his contribution helped to establish. He suffered an "attack of typhoid fever" from which he never recovered, and died on October 23, 1867, at the age of seventy-one.

Storer, an avowed Whig, had a history of activism for some time during his adult life. He had served the Sanford community as selectman and member of the school board, and for a year he acted as the postmaster of Springvale. He perhaps had been the leading citizen of Sanford when it came to support for the Union effort during the Civil War. Prior to his death, Storer "offered to erect a monument in memory of the soldiers at Sanford" who had fought in the Civil War. However, Sanford declined his offer because of specified "conditions" that likely involved the township assuming partial responsibility by raising matching funds.

A large crowd attended Storer's burial service, conducted October 25, 1867. As a final indication of the direction in which his religious patronage had moved, the funeral of the man who had been in his lifetime a Congregationalist was officiated by Davis and Day, Free Will Baptist ministers. Two weeks later, the *Morning Star* reported to the denomination that "[John Storer] was not nominally a member of the Free Baptist denomination, but his sympathies had been more and more identifying him with us as a people." The report continued that his "interest in the school which he really founded was very deep, and during the last weeks of his life he expressed great gratitude that God had permitted him to live to know that it [Storer College] had become a fact." Davis and Day formally represented the denomination at Storer's funeral, and several Free Will Baptists were in attendance. The congregation as a whole realized—even if from a distance—that John Storer was a man as "fixed as the hills" when it came to two things: executing good business practices and supporting those less fortunate than he. It would now be up to the denomination to make Storer's vision a reality, and it would be assisted in these efforts by a key contact in Washington, Senator William Pitt Fessenden.

WILLIAM PITT FESSENDEN, STORER COLLEGE'S ADVOCATE

William Pitt Fessenden was one of Storer's fellow Bowdoin alumni, and a financier and statesman. He was born in 1806 in New

Hampshire, but throughout his legal career he would be associated with the state of Maine. An 1823 graduate of Bowdoin College, Fessenden was admitted to the bar and then opened his first law practice in Portland, assisting his father Samuel, who was already well known for his abolitionist stance.

When the mission of organizing Storer College was undertaken, Fessenden assumed the role of financial administrator over Storer's bequest. As such, he was responsible for verifying that the Free Will Baptist commissioners indeed met all of the requirements established by Storer, including the timely collection and verifiable submission of matching funds. In the early stages of development of the mission, Fessenden also assisted Cheney

William Pitt Fessenden

toward his goal of acquiring the Harpers Ferry property.

On Thursday, April 19, 1867, Cheney and Fessenden attempted to meet with Secretary of War Edwin M. Stanton in pursuit of this goal. Unfortunately, Stanton had to cancel the meeting because he was detained by the "Ohio-returns." Although Stanton was not expected to return until the next day, Fessenden encouraged Cheney to remain until he had spoken with the secretary regarding "permanent" occupancy by the Free Will Baptists of the federal buildings on Camp Hill in Harpers Ferry. Keenly aware of Fessenden's political acumen, Cheney stayed to help press the cause.

Cheney also feared that if the conference with officials was deferred, the "delay would have been at the sacrifice of all" work toward the Shenandoah Mission and the promise of its educational enterprise. The Free Will Baptist-Home Mission Society simply ran the risk of missing the chance to secure the government buildings. Cheney and Fessenden wanted the matter settled before the next congressional adjournment. Cheney waited patiewhat ntly, if anxiously, for Stanton's return in order to make the next step. They agreed to appeal to General Oliver Otis Howard should the need arise. The Baptists' political sagacity and patience finally paid off when they were given verbal approval, in 1867, to occupy the buildings on Camp Hill. The matter was ultimately settled on December 15th, 1868, by an Act of Congress, although James Calder, a future college president, expressed certain reservations with the decision.

JAMES CALDER

On March 18, 1867, James Calder wrote to Nathan Brackett in Harpers Ferry, ostensibly to express regrets that the latter could not attend a church convention in Harrisburg, Pennsylvania. Speaking from the perspective of a college administrator, Calder then proceeded to the true point of his letter. He disagreed with the plan of the Home Mission Society's "board of corporators" to use "color" as a delineating factor for the school's educational mission. Calder emphatically stated, "This plan for a 'Colored College' does not strike me favorably. We, as a denomination, profess to be opposed to caste, and claim that all our institutions should be open to black students. Why should we now build a college from which white students shall be excluded? Away with all caste." He concluded "I fear this is a snare for us which the devil has moved a Congregationalist [Storer] to tempt us with," making an indirect reference to Storer's pledge. Nonetheless, Calder accepted the invitation to join the commission, and the commission ultimately benefited from Calder's background and varied experience.

SILAS CURTIS

While James Calder had expressed reservations about the exclusionary charter's language and legal descriptor "colored," Silas Curtis was more troubled about the problem of financing the ongoing missionary school project. He confided to Nathan Wood Brackett his anxiety, writing "our funds are becoming low & the prospect ahead for any increase is not very flattering." The Free Will Baptists had sent members of the denomination—North and South—specifically to collect donations for school support, but Curtis was worried about the lack of funds being generated. He shared his worries with Brackett, noting that "Bro.

Stockman is in the field as agent, but he does not appear to be getting much money—I think we shall not be able to employ so many teachers next year as we have this year & I hardly know how to pay these bills."

Curtis is notable not only for his attention to financial detail but also for his diligent pursuit of church expansion and humanitarian efforts. After the death of his only child, which occurred when he was pastor of the Free Will Baptist Church in Lowell, Massachusetts, Curtis began to direct his energies toward denominational expansion and enterprise. He was, in fact, the major impetus behind the denominational periodical the *Morning Star*, which acted as the nearly official voice of the Free Will Baptists. With three other like-minded ministers, Curtis convened an "educational convention," out of which grew the Education Society and Biblical School that supported the Baptists' "Southern enterprise" to effect "moral" and "Christian character" in the school while teaching literacy skills to freedmen and their families.

From 1839 to 1869, he served as corresponding secretary for the Free Will Baptist-Home Mission Society, a position of tremendous responsibility given the number of outlying ministers and missionaries working in the South. All information to and from mission teachers, preachers, mission stations and centers was transmitted through Silas Curtis. When the war ended, Curtis was one of the first Free Will Baptist emissaries to work in Virginia. Two years before Nathan Wood Brackett's formal appointment in 1867, Curtis was named "superintendent of the work among the freedmen, and afterwards visited the schools and mission stations in

Shenandoah Valley." In the history of Storer College, Curtis's name stands alongside those of Cheney, Brackett, and others.

Although he expressed some reservations about its establishment, as did James Calder, Curtis proved by his history of activism that he was nonetheless an early advocate for the "Southern enterprise" and the vanguard in the movement. On many levels, his concerns were indeed justified. Despite such reservations, however, the Home Mission Society proceeded with its plans. They set about selecting someone to take charge of operations at the Shenandoah mission, plus someone to act as superintendent of schools. The society and its commission collectively decided that the best combination to lead the project would be the Reverends Alexander Hatch Morrell and Nathan Cook Brackett.

The society sent Morrell to Harpers Ferry to "take charge of the missionary operations" at the Shenandoah Mission, while at the same time they officially appointed Brackett as superintendent of schools. From 1867 to 1880, Morrell functioned as the mission's religious administrator while Brackett coordinated educational activities and filled various administrative roles to ensure that "the church & school [would] be mutual auxiliaries" creating greater efficiency and increased resourcefulness.

ALEXANDER HATCH MORRELL

Alexander Hatch Morrell was selected by the society for his gifts of religious leadership and devotion, but especially for his broad appeal.

He was also known as a caring, sympathetic man interested in the welfare of others for whom he assumed spiritual responsibility, although he was never intrusive while shepherding his flocks. During revival meetings, he delivered powerful and yet sentimental sermons. His religious charisma made him a favorite with the elderly, the middle-aged, and even children, with whom he had a special rapport. Morrell's appeal to children gave him an advantage with the Home Mission Society. The commission therefore charged him to invigorate the mission's religious component, and provide spiritual sustenance for the Free Will Baptist-Home Mission Society's mission workers.

Morrell was personally inclined to go to Harpers Ferry, since he was an original member of the Commission For the Promotion of Education in the South. He was thus

Rev. A. H. Morrell.

acquainted with the operations in the valley, and his primary task was to organize churches in support of the mission. Some of his duties as the mission's religious leader also included regular reports to the denomination's *Morning Star* and *Freeman*, which were widely disseminated throughout New England, and the *Berkeley Union*, a local weekly newspaper published in bordering Berkeley County in Martinsburg. By such reports, it was

The Founding of Storer

hoped that Morrell would cultivate and maintain positive relationships with both local and distant communities regarding the denomination's work in the valley, by enlarging understanding for the Baptists' mission, progress, and needs.

By the time Alexander Morrell finally arrived in Harpers Ferry, the society had so sharply defined his duties that he knew exactly how to proceed with the work of the Shenandoah Mission, as did Nathan Wood Brackett. Morrell was given "oversight of the churches and people, giving much-needed instruction in all that pertains to social and religious life," which left Brackett and the mission teachers to concentrate on the mission schools and general educational development.

Within a year after moving to Harpers Ferry, however, Morrell was beset by an unknown illness. Morrell's leadership was a vital aspect of the mission center and the school network that it sponsored. Kate Anthony, an active member in the Woman's Home Missionary Society, asserted that Morrell was a special person "whose heart had been strongly drawn to the work [and] was sent to Harpers Ferry by the Home Mission Society to engage in special missionary efforts and build up Free Baptist churches." Despite his illness, during the thirteen years that he served as pastor and soliciting agent for the Free Will Baptist-Home Mission Society, the denomination at large concluded that "he performed a most useful work" for the Shenandoah Mission.

An 1861 United States Christian Commission station

NATHAN COOK BRACKETT

The commission's choice for superintendent came swiftly. Before June 10, 1867, Isaac Dalton Stewart communicated to Nathan Cook Brackett that the Home Mission Society had voted to elect him "Superintendent of Schools in the Shenandoah Valley for the year ensuing." The choice was a logical one, for Brackett had long been a devoted denominational laborer.

Brackett was born on July 28, 1836, in Phillips, Maine. He attended nearby Phillips High School and later the Maine State Seminary in Lewiston, where he met Oren Burbank Cheney, who had been a major impetus behind the "Southern enterprise" from its inception. After leaving the seminary, Brackett entered Dartmouth College, from which he graduated in 1864. From 1864 to 1865, following a short stint in South Carolina, he followed Sheridan's Union Army Corps wagons throughout the Shenandoah Valley and into Harpers Ferry as a representative of the United States Christian Commission.

In the Shenandoah Valley, Brackett's responsibilities were varied and—with so much to accomplish—seemingly never fulfilled. He transferred soldiers' pay—from both Confederate and Union forces—to the railroads' agents to ship back home to family members for safekeeping. He ministered to the troops. He observed, storing what he saw and heard and experienced, for future reference.

Although he worked tirelessly during this period, Brackett's greatest work was probably with the Shenandoah Mission after the war. Complementing his domestic mission in the Shenandoah Valley, Brackett was also a member of the Free Will Baptist Foreign Mission Board from 1878 to 1883. Additionally, he was a member of the General Conference Board and the Board of Corporators for the *Morning Star*. This publication, under the organizational aegis of the Free Will Baptist Printing Establishment, helped acquire vital financing for educational efforts in the Shenandoah Valley.

Rev. N. C. Brackett.

Brackett's devotion and commitment eventually cultivated respect. In 1821, he received official endorsement from one of West Virginia's premier educators, Dr. Carter Goodwin Woodson. Woodson, after teaching in the state for several years, complimented Brackett on "the successful work being accomplished there [at Storer College] under the direction of Dr. N. C. Brackett—[since it was] the only effort for secondary education for Negroes in the State" until the 1890 Morrill Act.

The mission school work was carried out faithfully by Brackett and the mission teacher cohort, although the superintendent's responsibilities were somewhat alleviated by the arrival of Alexander Morrell. Although Brackett was Maine-born and New

Concerned citizens with assigned agents pose outside of the United States Christian Commission

Hampshire-educated, he was in West Virginia long enough and worked for its interests with such fervor that he considered it his adopted state, and was buried in Harpers Ferry in 1910.

During 1864 to 1865, Brackett observed firsthand the partitioning of the newly organized state, as well as the geographical, social, economic, and political developments beginning to take shape there. Prepared or not, Brackett was thrust into the reality of Southern politics. The Southern sociopolitical setting forcibly shaped Brackett's mission school network, influenced the subsequent mission's organization, and contributed to the mission teachers' occasional social ostracization.

Thus it is small wonder that in 1867, when the commission considered candidates for superintendent of the new school, Brackett's name was virtually unchallenged. Simultaneously with being named superintendent, he received additional orders from the commission. In a letter received by the new superintendent on June 10, the Home Mission Society secretary, I. D. Stewart informed Brackett of several decisions made by the denomination. The society had voted to employ and sustain twelve permanent mission teachers. Brackett was required to implement and "arrange a system of tuition" for the 1868–69 school term "with discretion to remit to indigent pupils." Additionally, he was to ensure that mission teachers were not allowed "to remain in the Valley" between school terms. The last provision was intended to assure the physical safety and psychological resilience of the mission teachers. The society believed it best to send the mission teachers back to New England to recuperate among family and friends while at the same time to relate their experiences in the South to the denomination's various invested societies.

In quick succession, then, the denomination had chosen the people who would staff its schools and had begun the process of directing its work. However, the hardest part of the job—funding and creating the school itself—was yet to be accomplished. It had, however, begun with great fervor two months before when Brackett had been chosen superintendent.

FUNDING BEGINS IN EARNEST

In April 1867, Cheney met in Harrisburg with two other members of his organizational subcommittee, Calder and George Ball. Afterward, the trio proceeded to a meeting with Secretary Simon Cameron, in the War Department, from whom they sought political support as well as an opinion regarding the denomination's likelihood of securing the federal buildings on Camp Hill. During this meeting, it was decided that "at the proper time" when Calder believed that Governor Boreman of West Virginia was approachable, Calder was to request state aid amounting to $50,000. Since George Ball was from Buffalo, he became responsible for advancing a plea in New York on behalf of the educational commission to freedmen's aid and benevolent societies. Ball was specifically directed to contact Gerrit Smith, who subsequently donated $500 to the mission enterprise. A long-standing and "stalwart antislavery leader," Smith was known from the beginning of the antislavery movement for his New York speeches, which demanded unqualified emancipation, and he often used his private home as sanctuary for runaway slaves braving the long trip north in search of a new life.

That same month, with the commission's efforts off and running, Cheney posted a letter from Providence, Rhode Island, to Brackett, indicating that the Free Will Baptist-Home Mission Society "thought best to have some kind of an organization at once" in order to advance their strategies. Brackett was asked to read the secretary's notes on the meeting with Cameron and sign the conference paper for approval, returning it as soon as possible. Time was of the essence. In Washington, General Howard was also involved in the denomination's efforts, but likewise had developed plans for a normal school in the national district.

Howard ultimately would compete against the denomination for a share in philanthropists' funding for the District of Columbia's college named in his honor. Cheney had to ensure that the Free Will Baptist-Home Mission Society's plan was comparable to Howard's conception for a normal school in Washington—a school that would later become Howard University, instituted the same year as Storer in 1867.

Cheney contacted General Howard in Washington in order "to make his conditional subscription to this 'provisional committee' for the reason that he may die, or Johnson may remove him before we can get 'incorporated.' If he will make the subscription to us, we will give bonds for the safe keeping of funds" toward accumulating the necessary matched funds for the "Southern enterprise."

The paths of both men and both projects ultimately led to New York and Dr. Barnas Sears, director of the Peabody Education Fund. Cheney discussed several options with Sears, requesting that Sears forward a "Peabody Circular" to Brackett in Harpers Ferry. Like Howard, Cheney was specifically interested in Sears's requirements for normal school scholarships to support tuition and boarding costs. Sears informed Cheney of the particulars of the requirements and Brackett signed the commission's proposed school plan. Cheney next circulated the plan to Day, Knowlton, Curtis, Brewster, and Goodwin. Their signatures were presented first to "Bro. Storer" to verify that every effort and progress was being made to complete the stipulations of John Storer's detailed plan.

Fund-raising efforts continued unabated. The commission's secretary, Jonathan Brewster, forwarded Free Will Baptist-Home Mission Society circulars to Brackett outlining the duties and responsibilities of everyone involved in the enterprise. Brewster directed Brackett to "distribute [the circulars] to the persons for which they are intended." With funds increasing and the acquisition of the land nearing, the denomination's efforts moved closer to fruition. Nonetheless, some hurdles—primarily financial—remained. Periodically, in order to meet monthly payments, the commission was forced to "hire money personally." Cheney was among those who did so in order to help the school become a reality.

In May, after much discussion among members of the Home Mission Society, Curtis sent Brackett a letter from Concord, in which he expressed directly his desire for a normal school. Curtis wrote, "I am decidedly in favor of a normal school as soon as we can obtain a place without incurring a debt." It was Curtis's opinion that "no colleges nor universities for the Freedmen will be needed for years to come & we had better attend to their present needs—I would be glad enough of the property at Harper's Ferry if you consider that a good healthy location & we can get the property. I am in favor of getting all the Bureau will let us have—& all we can get—I should hope to secure the 10,000 of Mr. Storer."

The sum promised by Storer was indeed forthcoming, but in the meantime additional matching funds also were arriving. After learning that the Freedmen's Bureau would contribute $6,000 to their cause, George Day wrote to Brackett, claiming that this news is "like cold water to a thirsty soul . . . the news which you send is specially refreshing." Day, a stickler for detail, went on to inquire on "what basis or condition" the bureau was to contribute. "Can it be counted as a part of the $10,000 which we must secure in order to get Mr. Storer's donation," Day inquired, "or is it Gen. H's subscription on the basis mentioned to Bro. Cheney?" Still, Day was so elated about finally receiving the $6,000 check that he revealed to Brackett in a letter dated November 26 that he "really enjoyed handling that piece of paper when I thought of all it signified." Day also requested a copy of Storer's terms of bequest, the original of which was in Brackett's possession. At this point, a little over a month remained before the denomination would have to raise matching funds. As Day recounted to Brackett, "it

seems that we must have the $10,000 invested on or before the 1st of Jan'y. We shall of course try to see that there is no slip about the matter, if we have to raise the money ourselves & take subscriptions & notes for security."

When the Baptists had accumulated $10,000 in matching funds, the commission's treasurer, Ebenezer Knowlton, had to forward to Senator Fessenden in Washington a sworn affidavit to verify that the "amount of money was on hand & invested" in "a temporary Stock Company organized under the laws of West Virginia."

Ebenezer Knowlton, "Devoted to the Interest of Humanity"

A descendant of three generations of ministers, Ebenezer Knowlton was born in Pittsfield, New Hampshire, on December 6, 1815, directly into the Free Will Baptist faith. Knowlton's father, also named Ebenezer, had been converted during a September 12, 1799, revival at which the denominational founder, Benjamin Randal, was present. Knowlton's early religious upbringing in a household with three generations of ministers likely contributed to his ability to cultivate social and political allies. Therefore, when the Free Will Baptists devised their plan of education, his contributions were of a political nature. He was able to expedite the incorporation of the "body politic" for the Commission for the Promotion of Education in the South by applying his political know-how for the commission's task.

Knowlton's skill as a legislator become so renowned that in 1869 he was courted by the Maine Republican Party Convention as a gubernatorial candidate. Knowlton declined, his decision swayed most likely by his educational responsibilities and by a fear that politics would distract him from his religious activities. He went on to serve the denomination as president of the Free Will Baptist-Home Mission Society, a "corporator" of the Free Will Baptist Printing Establishment, and primary moderator for many Free Will Baptist General Conferences. His name appears frequently in Storer College records, and he remained active with the college in Harpers Ferry until sometime around 1871–72, when ill health most likely prohibited further work. Until that time, Knowlton supported denominational efforts by exercising his political clout and expertise, which were aptly paired with George Day's experienced background in legal policy.

Rev. Ebenezer Knowlton.

GEORGE TIFFANY DAY, A PROPENSITY FOR "INCESSANT TOIL"

Like many of his fellow Free Will Baptists, George Tiffany Day was intimately involved in the most important social and reform movements of his day. On December 2, 1859, as John Brown was being executed in Charles Town, West Virginia, Day was among several speakers to address a large public assembly in Providence, Rhode Island. There he prayed not only for the condemned man's soul but also for the impending national strife that he so strongly sensed was to follow Brown's execution. An orator, minister, essayist, and published author, Day was regarded as both a great preacher and political force who had appeared several times before the Rhode Island Legislature. One of the topics on which he was particularly vocal was that of emancipation. From 1858 to 1859, he "made several speeches before the Legislature on the Colored School bill" proposal in his capacity as a respected community advocate.

Rev. G. T. Day.

Due to his propensity for "incessant toil"—from early in his career he was known for working until he reached a state of utter exhaustion—Day was forced to periodically convalesce. In February 1864, just three months before Cheney and Brackett planned to leave Maine to join the United States Christian Commission in the South, Day left Rhode Island ahead of Cheney and Brackett for Virginia. There he worked for a period as a representative of the Christian Commission and superintendent of

Civil War field operations of the USCC in Virginia

Southern schools. It is possible that Day and Brackett were assigned to the same commission corps, or at the least crossed paths along the way. Cheney was also involved with the commission at the time, but according to his wife Emeline Burlingame-Cheney, he was then working out of the national headquarters in Washington, D.C.

Day paired his policy know-how with Brewster, and began soliciting funds for the commission on behalf of the college. Together both men played a vital role in directing the institution's early financial matters. In 1867, while Day was the acting editor of the *Morning Star*, it fell to him to publish the death notice of Storer's benefactor, John Storer, on October 23.

JONATHAN MCDUFFEE BREWSTER, PASTOR AND SUPERINTENDENT

Jonathan McDuffee Brewster was involved with the effort that led to the creation of Storer College through his success at soliciting funds to support the "Southern enterprise." He was raised on a family farm in Wolfborough, New Hampshire, and in 1860 graduated from Dartmouth College, as did Nathan Wood Brackett four years later. After leaving Dartmouth, Brewster pursued theological studies in New Hampton and Andover, Massachusetts. He completed his ministerial training in 1863 as pastor of the church in Springvale, Maine, during the height of civil conflict. In December 1864, he was officially ordained into the ministry. That same year, after a convincing conversation with William Burr, Jonathan Brewster became assistant editor of the *Morning Star*.

Between the years 1869 and 1871, as the work at Storer College became more intensive and time consuming, Brewster was also serving as pastor to churches in both Fairport, New York, and North Scituate, Rhode Island. He was later elected superintendent of public schools for the latter region. Since Brewster served as both pastor and superintendent in the North Scituate community, he was a well-known and prominent citizen. Brewster's high-profile activities in the religious and educational arenas gave him a leadership role in the movement to provide education for freedmen. His experience helped to diversify the commission and inform its

Jonathan McDuffee Brewster

understanding for freedmen's education as it proceeded to solicit funds in support of its school plan. From 1872 to 1882, he participated in several important activities on behalf of the Free Will Baptists. First, he was appointed clerk of the Rhode Island Association. In 1875, he became an original "corporator" of the Free Will Baptist Printing Establishment. With a high level of missionary zeal, he served on both the domestic and foreign mission boards (acting on the Executive Board of Directors for the latter). He was elected to several terms on the Board of Trustees for Storer College, which grew out of the original Commission for the Promotion of Education in the South. Brewster's activism touched on many reformist issues of the period. Just prior to his death on June 2, 1882, he was actively engaged with the Committee of the Rhode Island Woman's Suffrage Association, operating as an advocate for women's voting rights in that state.

GEORGE HARVEY BALL

Unlike Brewster and most of his Free Will Baptist peers "stationed" in New England, George Harvey Ball can claim wide-ranging places of residence and a unique educational background. Although his parents were native New Englanders—both were residents of Massachusetts—Ball was born on December 7, 1819, in the Canadian province of Nova Scotia, in the inlet township of Sherbrooke, near Wine Harbor. In 1836, when Ball was still a youngster, his family moved to the Ohio wilder-

ness, where until the age of twenty he was home-schooled by his mother. The young Ball studied until ten o'clock each evening, preparing his lessons and working diligently, so that before long he found himself teaching other children in his community, first unofficially and then in a frontier schoolhouse.

During the next several years, Ball's career took him in many directions. At the Ashtabula Quarterly Meeting, he was granted a license to preach, and he either instituted churches or ministered to congregations throughout Ontario, New York, and Rhode Island. Ball became principal of the Geauga Seminary, where he taught and influenced numerous students, among them future U.S. president James Abram Garfield.

Rev. G. H. Ball, D. D.

Ball's legacy includes his role in the establishment of two denominational higher education institutions: Hillsdale College in Michigan and Storer College in Harpers Ferry. His organizational skills were an asset to the Commission for the Promotion of Education in the South, although his religious work often took him far afield. As a member of the Foreign Mission and Free Will Baptist Conference Boards, for example, he represented the Free Will Baptists at the General Baptist Conference held in England in 1883. Moreover, his other activities were equally diverse. During the 1870s, he served as editor for two denominational publications, the *Morning Star* and the *Baptist Union*. During the height of the postwar debates, Ball's experiences as an editor prompted him to publish several books, articles, and essays for other New England religious and secular presses.

ISAAC DALTON STEWART

Isaac Dalton Stewart, the author of *The History of the Freewill Baptists*, was born in Warner, New Hampshire, just outside of Concord two days before Christmas 1817. Of Scots-English ancestry, Stewart lived with his parents and five siblings on a two hundred-acre ancestral farm with a vista that "commanded a wide prospect extending into more than twenty towns." Stewart's educational background is indicative of his family's social status. He attended school in a district that boasted "eighteen teachers, six members of the Legislature and one governor of the state" among a class of twenty-five scholars.

After attending Hopkinton Academy for a period, Stewart left New Hampshire for Ohio. He lived there until 1838, first teaching before deciding ultimately upon law as a profession. Before long, though, his plans would change. First, he returned to New Hampshire, where he taught and continued his studies at Henniker Academy. Then he moved to New Jersey, where he also taught briefly at Scotch Plains near Westfield, in Union County. In 1841, Stewart enrolled in the

Biblical School located at North Parsonfield, Maine, under the tutelage of Reverend Smart, but he eventually transferred to the New Hampton Theological School, which was operated by the Baptists. In 1842, Stewart became the principal of the Henniker Academy, where among his pupils he counted James W. Patterson, who was later elected to the United States Congress.

Rev. I. D. Stewart, D. D.

He returned to New Hampshire in 1867, however, just in time for John Storer to appoint him as one of the nine-member Commission for the Promotion of Education in the South. Stewart made every effort and "strenuous exertion" to ensure that the "conditions of Mr. Storer's will" were met within the specified time limits. Stewart supported the commission financially and politically. He also served as recording secretary for the Free Will Baptist-Home Mission Society, as well as a member of it executive committee. He was secretary of the Anniversary Convention, a member of the Education Society and a member of the Board of Trustees for both Storer and Hillsdale colleges. He so strongly believed in the denomination's "Southern enterprise" that he committed to use his ancestral farm either as collateral or even for sale if need be in order to acquire the matching funds to meet Storer's terms of contract. In order to prevent the failure of the denomination's Southern venture, Stewart had pledged his entire property on behalf of the institution.

CHARLES HOWARD, PHILANTHROPIST

Charles Howard was brother to Oliver Otis Howard, and served as a trustee to the university that still bears his family's surname before becoming involved with the creation of the school in Harpers Ferry. It was important to both Howard brothers that a school for freedmen be instituted in the District of Columbia, particularly since in preceding decades "the unfinished and desecrated capital" had been blemished by the presence of "slavemongers" and "slave drivers" marching chained, marching slaves through the streets. Northerners visiting the capital city during those decades were forced to face the reality of the slave trade in the very heart of the nation to their horror and chagrin. Until 1850, Washington had served as the collection site, or slave "depot" for slaves in transit waiting to be "sold down the river," temporarily held in the capital until boarded on trains and ships destined for slave states and domestic distribution. The institution of slavery was not banned from the capital city until 1862, after the Civil War's onset. By that time, as slaves began to equate war with liberty and liberty with full emancipation, they had begun to make the trek northward toward freedom.

As the slaves gravitated northward to border states, Charles Howard was there to lend his administrative support. Howard had become familiar with the Harpers Ferry area, having traversed across it during the war

years. Later, he probably again visited the region for the Freedmen's Bureau when his older brother, Oliver Otis, needed dependable government representatives in potentially incendiary regions.

When Charles Howard agreed to become a member of the Board of Trustees for Storer College, he was also a trustee for Howard University. This practical experience was quite useful for the fledgling institution. He provided a keen sense for the grander scheme of things for the school in Harpers Ferry. He was closely linked with Howard University due to his older brother, Oliver Otis, who was appointed president of the university in 1869. Charles Howard's participation with the administrative board at Storer College was fortunate for the school since it is likely that he was familiar with educational structures at Howard University, which had been granted provisional charter the same year as Storer College, in 1867. Charles Howard then operated as an educational advisor, as well as a trustee for the college.

His primary focus was with the school's finances (likely in correspondence with the Freedmen's Bureau) during a time when the Baptists needed his insight and input. Regardless, Howard's early involvement with the school in the capital city made him a tireless advocate for similar institutions, particularly the one in nearby Harpers Ferry.

DANIEL AMES AND MARY CLEMMER

In a June 17, 1867 letter to Nathan Cook Brackett, Jonathan Brewster identified Daniel Ames as "a member of the committee to raise funds" and indicates that Brackett should thereafter "explain to [Ames] the nature of his duties." Ames had served, for a brief period, as principal of a boys' school in New Jersey and had been a congregational minister in both New York and Minnesota prior to his arrival in Harpers Ferry. In Harpers Ferry, he joined the Baptists' Commission for the Promotion of Education in the South after the war's end.

It was while working in New York that Ames met his future wife, Utica native Mary E. Clemmer, a well-educated woman who had attended the Westfield Academy in Massachusetts and had embarked on a career in journalism. Clemmer and her husband in due course relocated to Harpers Ferry, where Daniel Ames took a position with the federal government and their lives became embroiled with events leading up to the Civil War. They did not have long to wait before their ferry community was affected by the rising tensions. On April 17, 1861, "despite western admonitions" and "without waiting" for the "required ratification by the people in the spring elections on May 23," Governor Letcher adopted a secession ordinance. Governor Letcher rushed to dispatch troops to

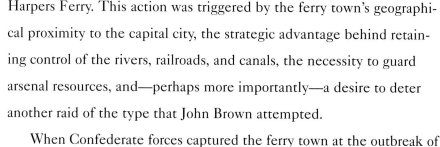

Mary E. Clemmer

Harpers Ferry. This action was triggered by the ferry town's geographical proximity to the capital city, the strategic advantage behind retaining control of the rivers, railroads, and canals, the necessity to guard arsenal resources, and—perhaps more importantly—a desire to deter another raid of the type that John Brown attempted.

When Confederate forces captured the ferry town at the outbreak of war, Ames was thus working there and living peacefully with his wife, but he was considered a risk because of his association with the government. As a result, the Ames were taken into custody by Confederate guardsmen and imprisoned. At the time, Daniel Ames had been working for the federal government in Harpers Ferry as a self-described "storekeeper." Nonetheless, despite his caretaker mission at the start of the war, he later proved himself as valuable as any of his fellow Free Will Baptists in securing the success of the Harper's Ferry mission. For her part, Mary Clemmer eventually became the highest paid female journalist of her time. She was in Harpers Ferry, in 1865, when the first mission teacher cohort arrived by train to the Shenandoah Mission.

Since Daniel Ames was located in Harpers Ferry when the Storer bequest was preferred, he likely acted as local liaison for the Commission for the Promotion of Education in the South. It is clear as well that the commission depended on its federal relationships to a moderate degree to promote its best interests, and Ames had the contacts and patronage ties needed for success.

EDWARD A. STOCKMAN, GENEROUS PATRON

In 1865, Edward A. Stockman was among the first ministers hired by the Free Will Baptists to venture south, yet his work with the mission school at times proved dissatisfying to the group. In fact, of all the men involved in the enterprise, Stockman received harsh criticism for his inability to work effectively and consistently toward raising funds, one of his primary responsibilities. Yet, when considering the immediate fallout from the war, Stockman was working at a disadvantage. He was, after all, trying to counteract strong and lingering Confederate sympathies and his position was made even weaker by Andrew Johnson's Reconstruction policies.

Initially commissioned by Silas Curtis to organize relief efforts and institute churches, Stockman traveled to a large plantation six miles outside Beaufort, North Carolina, where—before his arrival—the "colored people" had actually begun to organize on their own a Baptist "settlement [and] a meeting house [with] a colored preacher." Unlike these hardy souls, however, most freed Southerners were reluctant to take such action because they feared President Johnson betrayed their emancipation by creating policies that discouraged the assistance of relief workers, while encouraging lawlessness.

After working in Beaufort, Stockman moved to Hilton Head, South Carolina, where he remained to organize a church until further "directions" were given by Curtis. As corresponding secretary for the Home Mission Society, Curtis had other plans for Stockman, which he dis-

cussed in a letter to Brackett. "If you think [Stockman's] labors with you in the Shenandoah Valley or the district you have assigned to you, as a preacher and missionary would be for the advancement of the cause we are laboring to promote, please so inform me." Curtis's decision to place Stockman in Harpers Ferry was motivated by a desire to consolidate a Free Will Baptist power base. As he noted in a letter, he urgently wanted "to concentrate freedmen's mission work to someone locally, instead of having it scattered so far apart" amid continuing instability.

Curtis was concerned about keeping Stockman not only employed, but also out of danger. Stationed as he was for a period in South Carolina, where the situation remained unstable, Stockman faced peril as a result of his work on behalf of the freedmen. "[Stockman] is our missionary to Beaufort," Curtis pleaded to Brackett, "& he informs me that the consequence of the policy of the government in pardoning the Rebs and restoring to them their property at Beaufort & the Sea Islands the Freedmen are leaving Beaufort in such numbers that soon there will be none of any consequence in the place" to which to minister or educate. Since Johnson's policy essentially granted former Confederates a pardon in exchange for a simple pledge of loyalty to the Union, Southern states grew exceedingly dangerous for reformers.

Before being placed in Harpers Ferry, Stockman returned to the American Missionary Association's offices in New York for a brief respite while Curtis determined his next move. Suggesting that Stockman was a "good preacher & good business man" and "a man of good judgment," Curtis proposed to Brackett that "he can board in your club and travel out & do mission work, visit, distribute books & tracts, visit schools, preach & etc. to good advantage & the advancement of our mission there." Ultimately, Silas Curtis would perhaps rue his praise.

During mid-January 1866, the Free Will Baptist-Home Mission Society decided to send Stockman to assist Nathan Wood Brackett in Harpers Ferry. Upon arrival, Stockman reported to Brackett for his orders and "plan of operation." While Brackett was ordered to remain as "Superintendent of the mission & schools in the district," Curtis suggested that he "consult with [Stockman], & decide where & how he had better labor for the present: & [. . .] propose any plan of operation for Bro. Stockman which you may think best after looking around & conversing with him; & we will give our approval or disapproval and directions as we think best after learning facts from you."

Stockman was given a huge responsibility—fund-raising. During the fall of 1867, Stockman was noted as being "in the west," frantically collecting personal notes from friends, family, and supporters of the Free Will Baptists in order to amass the necessary cash capital required by Fessenden in his capacity as legal guardian of the Storer bequest. At this time, Brackett learned that Stockman had been pledged up to $1,500 in notes for the enterprise. Yet, Curtis believed that his efforts were insufficient. At one point, he suggested to Brackett, "I propose sending Bros. Dunjee & Keys" to replace Stockman the following year to collect notes, meet with church-goers, and solicit support for the school. Concurring with Curtis, Day claimed that "Bro. Stockman is doing less than ever in the agency, & proposes to give it up if we wish him to. I suppose he may be planning to give up the H.M. agency altogether, & perhaps take a pastorate. We are trying to get two other men at work, & hope to do something before Jan'y 1."

Early in 1868, Stockman was still collecting "notes" from individuals who had lent the denomination cash to make the January 1, 1868, deadline for raising matching funds. Although frantic, Stockman's efforts must have fallen short for the following spring (1869), Curtis reported to Brackett that Stockman "does not appear to be getting much money" to help finance the school. Eventually, Stockman would abandon the "Southern enterprise" in order to organize a church of his own in New England.

JOSEPH T. HOKE, AN "ACTIVE PROMOTER"

A native of Martinsburg, where he was born in 1835, Joseph T. Hoke was the only Berkeley County representative appointed to the Commission for the Promotion of Education in the South. Well-known and respected throughout the region, Hoke was barely thirty years old when he vigilantly assisted the Free Will Baptists with the charter of Storer College. Later he was elected to the Senate in the West Virginia

Legislature. Nonetheless, Hoke and his family incurred sharp criticism from some elements of the Martinsburg community because they boarded mission teachers.

Well-educated and politically sophisticated, Hoke was a confirmed Unionist who would not be deterred by the grumbling of the disaffected. At a young age, he had left Virginia for Illinois to be educated at the Rock River Seminary. From there, he had attended Ohio's Oberlin College, which had a reputation for being a "friend of the oppressed" and was known for its work early in the nineteenth century with Native Americans and Negroes.

HON. JOSEPH T. HOKE, LL. D.

Exposure to Oberlin's social philosophy perhaps broadened Hoke's perspective. Consequently, he decided to attend Hillsdale College, the Free Will Baptist school in Michigan. He graduated from Hillsdale in 1860. In 1864 he graduated from Michigan University with a law degree. Hoke returned that same year to Martinsburg, where he was admitted to the Berkeley County Bar in the new state of West Virginia.

Primed to be an activist, Hoke immediately became immersed in local affairs, which helped involve him in the Storer enterprise. In 1864, he ran for public office and, at the age of twenty-nine, was elected Berkeley County's prosecuting attorney. In 1864, he began publishing the *Berkeley Union*, a pro-Unionist newspaper that became the weekly newspaper published in Martinsburg (although the *Martinsburg Gazette* had been in operation since 1799).

Hoke's liberal views were countered by the *Martinsburg New Era*—a conservative, Confederate-imbued newspaper—that was founded the next year. At one point, the two newspapers waged an editorial war regarding the mission school. The *New Era* cautioned local citizens, or "the elite of our place," against offering a "cordial welcome" to the New England schoolteachers, who had been commonly referred to in the area as "nigger teachers." In an editorial in the *Union*, Hoke—who was an acting commissioner at the school—responded to Charles Faulkner's "slight fling" not only on behalf of the mission teachers but also on behalf of the Free Will Baptists' "Southern enterprise" as a whole. Charles Faulkner had been such a notorious Confederate that the state and federal governments were prompted to demand his incarceration and proscription for a period.

Hoke was a constant campaigner and political office holder. In 1866, he vied for a senatorial seat in the West Virginia Legislature, was elected, and then was reelected for two subsequent terms, in 1868 (when he served as the Judiciary Committee's chairman) and again in 1886. Later he accepted an appointment to the Fifth Judicial Circuit. During a twelve-year period, Hoke attended the Republican National Convention three times—in 1868, 1872, and 1880—as West Virginia's elected delegate. Defeated as a congressional candidate in 1880, Hoke later was elected to the Third Judicial Circuit, after which he was

"Oren B. Cheney, Silas Curtis, Ebenezer Knowlton, George T. Day, Jonathan M. Brewster, Nathan C. Brackett, George Goodwin, James Colder, George H. Ball, Alexander H. Morrell, Isaac D. Stewart, Charles H. Howard, Daniel J. Young, Daniel Ames, Edward A. Stockman, John O'Donnell, and their associates, be and they are hereby created a body politic and corporate, by the name and style of 'The President and Trustees of Storer College,' an institution of learning for the education of youth, without distinction of race or color, at or near Harper's Ferry, in the county of Jefferson, . . .[the board] shall have power to establish in said college such departments and courses of study as they may elect; they shall have power to confer such degrees as are usually conferred by colleges and universities established for the education of youth, and they shall be and they are hereby invested with all the rights, powers, privileges and immunities incident to similar corporations and institutions."

—Final draft of the Charter Committee of the Commission for the Promotion of Education in the South

appointed consul to St. John's in the Canadian province of New Brunswick. Hoke's sense of justice and political radicalism fueled the West Virginia Legislature's political engines, so that eventually a state charter of incorporation was granted to The Commission for the Promotion of Education in the South. It meant that the state officially recognized Storer College as "an institution of learning for the education of youth."

This occurred during the West Virginia Legislature's Sixth Session, held in Wheeling in March 1868 while Hoke served as a state senator. The pursuit of incorporation began in January of that year, when Isaac Stewart wrote to Brackett requesting a copy of the "Charter for Storer College that we may have a guide in the draft of the one we are to ask from the Legislature." In early February, the Commission for the Promotion of Education in the South received a report from its Charter Committee, whose goal was "to procure a charter for Storer College from the Legislature of West Virginia." When the three-member Charter Committee—Cheney, Knowlton, and Calder—presented their draft of the charter to the Commission, it generated "various suggestions." The assembled commission voted that the "whole subject of obtaining a charter from West Virginia be left with the Committees, appointed by the Commission and the Corporation of Storer College." Cheney, Knowlton, and Calder were expected to "confer with Mr.

Fessenden" not only regarding the charter of the school but also on "his returning possession of the $10,000 donated to the Commission by Mr. Storer," and "to secure the passage of a bill by congress granting to the Commission certain Government property at Harper's Ferry."

When the school's charter was presented in the State Legislature, there was "intense and violent opposition," largely over inclusion of the phrase "without distinction of race, or color." These words were a reflection of Cheney's moral objection to exclusionary language. Hoke served not just as a member of the commission but also as local legal counsel for the Baptists through the debate. As the question of Storer's charter moved through the legislative process, he realized that the voting margin was likely to be narrow, so as the date for the legislative roll call approached, he "carefully watched" the "progress of events." The Baptists anxiously awaited Hoke's reports. He knew that his direct affiliation with the Commission for

> Brackett, Knowlton, and Calder had worked steadily to create the charter, but when the question of incorporation of the college reached the legislature, it was Hoke's political sagacity that proved vital to the Free Will Baptists.

the Promotion of Education in the South would deny his vote on the question of Storer's charter since he would be an interested party. Therefore, Hoke hastily (if only temporarily) resigned his appointment to the Baptist "commission" in the final hour before the legislature's representatives cast their votes and thus ensured that his own senatorial vote could be cast.

Hoke's resignation was a necessary stratagem. His act allowed him to "cast the decisive vote, for the success of the measure turned upon his foresight and the Act passed by . . . one [vote]." On March 3, 1868, the charter passed in Wheeling. After the vote, Senator Hoke immediately resumed his appointment to the Baptist Commission, which afterward convened as the Storer College Board of Trustees. Storer College had been incorporated. After the vote, the senator immediately resumed his appointment to the Baptist commission, which afterward convened as the Storer College Board of Trustees. Storer College had been incorporated.

Charles Faulkner

Storer's Early Days
The Campus and the Curriculum

Storer College collage

THE OPENING OF STORER COLLEGE

The Commission for the Promotion of Education in the South convened as the school's first Board of Trustees when Storer College opened it doors to students on October 3, 1867, under provisional authority in compliance with the original Baptist plan and Storer's contract. The formal governing structure included two executive officers, a five-member executive board, and a Board of Trustees consisting of twenty-one members. Calder, the newly elected president of Hillsdale College, also consented to be the first president of Storer's Board of Trustees—a logical choice given his years of educational experience and his ability to organize a college governing board. Nathan Brackett served as both secretary and treasurer. The Executive Board members were the Reverend J. W. Dunjee, Dr. George H. Ball, and the Honorable Stephen P. Morrill.

The Board of Trustees, a geographically and professionally diverse group, hailed from as far north as Maine, as far south as Virginia, as far west as Illinois, and as easterly as Massachusetts. Trustees included Dr. Oren Burbank Cheney, Honorable Ebenezer Knowlton, Reverend Jonathan Brewster, Honorable George Goodwin, Reverend Isaac Dalton Stewart, Reverend Daniel Ames, Honorable John O'Donnell, Reverend Silas Curtis, Dr. George Tiffany Day, Reverend Anthony H. Morrell, General Charles H. Howard, Reverend Edward Stockman, Honorable Joseph T. Hoke, Reverend T. J. Furgerson, and Henry Houke. To this distinguished board was added Anne S. Dudley, the first woman to serve on the Baptist college's Board of Trustees. Dudley's appointment truly indicates the degree to which the Free Will Baptists were dedicated to breaking boundaries.

The Free Will Baptists' primary mission in the South had been accomplished, both figuratively and literally. With Storer's seed money officially bequeathed to them on January 1, 1868, the Baptists got their "Southern enterprise" underway. The college's founders had succeeded in translating the freedmen's physical emancipation to the freedom to pursue an education. Higher education truly opened to the former slaves opportunities that had been withheld for far too long in the South. Storer College was—at long last—a reality.

THE CAMPUS, THE BUILDINGS, AND THE SECONDARY CURRICULUM, 1867–84

Storer College opened its doors in October 1867 with an initial enrollment of only nineteen students. All of these scholars had enrolled under the direction of a teacher trained in Maine, Miss Martha W. L. Smith. Barely three months later, however, the number of students had risen to thirty-six, and by the time the school's charter was officially granted on March 3 of the following year, seventy-five students were in attendance. Storer's early exponential growth made it plain that the Free Will Baptists must speed the physical development of the campus in order to meet the needs of a growing student population. The college was housed in four buildings set on seven acres in Harpers Ferry. These structures were originally built for use by armory officers, and were granted for Baptist use by the U.S. government.

The Physical Plant

Four main structures formed the physical nucleus of Storer College. The seven acres upon which they stood had served as part of the original triangular 125-acre headquarters of the United States Armory since June 15, 1796, when President George Washington established the arsenal in Harpers Ferry at the strategic confluence of the Potomac and Shenandoah rivers. After nearly a hundred years of service, the "four large, brick mansions" owned by the federal government at the summit of Camp Hill had seen better days.

Storer's Early Days

Originally the homes of the armory's administrative officers—the superintendent, the superintendent's clerk, the paymaster, and the paymaster's clerk—the structures had been damaged significantly during the Civil War. The Free Will Baptists, however, believed that the old buildings, no matter how war-torn, were of "inestimable value." In 1865, the federal government was persuaded to temporarily "loan" one of those buildings, the Lockwood House, to Brackett so that he could begin his "school work" in the region. It was not long, however, before Storer College outgrew its original, cramped home and the Free Will Baptists began to shape plans for expansion of their new campus.

Lockwood House was the first home of Storer College, but it was quickly found to be too small and too dilapidated to give sufficient shelter during the harsh winter months common to northeastern West Virginia. In September 1867, a year after the school had taken up residence in Lockwood House, the Freedmen's Bureau donated $500 for

This is a picture of Nathan and Louise Brackett (on left) posing outside Old Lincoln Hall with students including two mission teachers (on right), possibly Dudley, Stowers, or Smith.

the express purpose of funding needed repairs to the structure. This funding provided stopgap measures to help the school's residents combat the winter weather, but it did nothing to give them more room. The need for expansion of the facilities remained pressing. At the same time, the three other former government buildings on top of the Camp Hill site were vacant. Could they also be loaned to the college—or better yet, purchased, wondered the Free Will Baptists? It was an issue that the vigilant Cheney was already attempting to address.

Four months after his initial meeting with Storer to secure the bequest, Cheney traveled to Washington, where he received the promise of a $6,000 donation from the Freedmen's Bureau to serve as seed money for the matching funds required by Storer's arrangement. With funding on the horizon, Cheney turned his sights toward acquiring the Camp Hill property. He arranged to meet with U.S. Secretary of

War Stanton, William Pitt Fessenden, and, later, James A. Garfield, for whom he outlined the Free Will Baptists' plans and their desperate need for additional space. He broached the topic of the Camp Hill property, but he immediately sensed his listeners' ambivalence. Because no government official could guarantee Baptist occupation of the government site in Harpers Ferry, Cheney thought it best to devise an alternate plan in the event that the denomination was denied permanent occupancy of the Camp Hill buildings. With Cheney's personal assistance, the nearly 150-acre Smallwood Farm, located along the Bolivar Heights summit, was purchased as a potential alternative site for the college, with the deed of sale recorded by the Jefferson County clerk on June 18, 1867.

Although it would be retained as collateral to ensure the institution's financial security, the Smallwood Farm was not destined to become the home of Storer College. Eventually, the government moved beyond indecision on the Camp Hill property. On December 3, 1868, the US Congress granted the denomination the right to provisionally occupy all four government buildings on seven acres atop Camp Hill. This was fifteen months after the college accepted its first official entry-level class of nineteen students under the chartered name of Storer College. Then, on December 15, 1868, after the college was incorporated by the West Virginia State Legislature, the War Department published notice that the lands were to be sold at public auction. This sale would enable Storer to obtain permanent deed to the Camp Hill site.

By 1868, the four physical structures and the land on which they were built were valued at $30,000. After several weeks of mandatory public advertisement "in one of the principal newspapers in each of the cities of Washington, New York, and Cincinnati for sixty days prior to the sale," the government properties were sold at public auction over a three-day period.

As a result of this sale, the Free Will Baptists assumed ownership of four dilapidated buildings—Lockwood House, formerly the paymaster's quarters (Building 32); Brackett House, formerly the superintendent's clerks' quarters (Building 31); Morrell House, formerly the paymaster's clerk's quarters (Building 30); and Anthony House (Anthony Memorial Hall), formerly the superintendent's quarters (Building 25). After the deed received the official "War Department Seal" from the Secretary of War, the document was notarized in the "District of Columbia, City of Washington," whereby "the Secretary of War [then was] authorized and directed to convey by deed to Storer College, an institution of learning chartered by the State of West Virginia all those portions of aforesaid property . . . buildings with lots on which they stand, numbered thirty, thirty one and thirty two and also building numbered twenty five . . . ." The deed, which conveyed all four buildings plus acreage, was then entrusted to Thomas A. Moore, clerk of the County Court in the County of Jefferson, West Virginia, to be recorded in the county's Book of Deeds on December 15, 1869. The "Bargain and Sale" of these government properties in

Harpers Ferry was specifically directed to aid "religious, charitable and town purposes" after the war's close.

The Free Will Baptists were given special consideration for the "bargain and sale" of the four government buildings. This is due to the political sagacity of Cheney, Brackett, Knowlton, Calder, and others, with earlier political assistance from Howard, Fessenden, Cameron, Garfield, Hoke, and Senator Wiley, another West Virginia political ally who joined in the early efforts. The structures formed the initial campus of the "Southern enterprise" in which the Free Will Baptists were already so heavily invested. Before long, the buildings would be joined on Camp Hill by additional structures that had to be erected to serve the college's expanding population. These four buildings formed the core of the new college, and played an indispensable role in shaping the growth of the institution.

Lockwood House

The Lockwood House, as the structure later became known, was originally the site of a smaller building, that from 1819 to 1847 served first as the home of Captain John H. Hall. Hall was a gunsmith and inventor from Yarmouth, Maine, who arrived in Harpers Ferry in 1817. After a series of lucrative experiments,

Hall's pursuit led to the "Hall Breechloading Flintlock Rifle and Pistol." The government initially erected two buildings, later known as "Hall's Rifle Works" for Hall's usage on Virginus Island in the middle of the Shenandoah River.

Eventually Hall was named assistant armorer to the federal armory under Colonel James Stubblefield. Stubblefield was the armory's superintendent until 1829, during the armory's major time of growth, when Stubblefield also hired four teachers and instituted a school for "the

Lockwood House

education of his employees' children." After Stubblefield and Hall left the area, Archibald M. Kitzmiller, clerk to the armory superintendent then occupied Lockwood House. Kitzmiller was later, in 1859, one of two hostages that John Brown dispatched to negotiate a truce with federal agents.

After 1847, the smaller building was razed and a larger one constructed that would eventually house the armory's superintendent and paymaster, and still later be developed as Storer's main classroom building, chapel location, and administrative office. The initial house, which measured fifty-six by forty feet, was a single-story brick structure, complete with east and west porticoes, and was seated atop an elevated limestone basement (perhaps in an effort to prevent water damage from the area's underground springs). An eighteen- by twenty-foot brick outbuilding was included, along with a large cistern that was meant to ensure a generous water supply for its inhabitants. In 1858, a second story was added to the structure and two years later, government plans were authorized for a new horse stable to replace an "old rough cast stable." The stable's construction was delayed by the outbreak of the Civil War.

After the onset of war, the armory property was occupied at different times by various military representatives, who—along with the later religious representatives—became inextricably connected not only with the history of the "sleepy pre-war town" but also with select physical structures. For example, the former home of the superintendent's clerk bears not his name, nor that of his successors, but that of Civil War

General Henry Hayes Lockwood, who lived in the government house for a scant three months in 1863, while preparing a brigade for the Battle of Gettysburg. The war ensured Lockwood's connection to Harpers Ferry. A dispatch from General Meade, dated August 1, 1863, ordered Lockwood's garrison to defend the Potomac River from Harpers Ferry, West Virginia, to Williamsport, Maryland, "in view of the probability of the return of Lee or a part of his army into Maryland. It was part of Meade's strategy to impede Lee's progress up and down the valley, knowing that Lee was quite familiar with the terrain in that area.

After Lockwood vacated the ferry town, General Philip Henry Sheridan, who commanded the Army of the Shenandoah, to which Brackett had been assigned as a USCC field delegate, sequestered the government house on Camp Hill in 1864. When Brackett was in Harper's Ferry with Sheridan, he helped a young woman named Julia Mann. She operated a school for slave refugees in Lockwood House from the winter months of 1864 through the first months of 1865, just before the Appomattox Surrender.

Without question, Julia Mann's uncle, educational reformer Horace Mann, whose democratic vision and republican ideology ignited the Common School Movement in America, influenced his niece. Perhaps his belief in "universal education" had even inspired her willingness to relocate to the Shenandoah Valley on behalf of educating war refugees. Brackett acquired a heightened sense for the degree of refugee duress and also likely witnessed the mounting social prejudice against the young schoolteacher during these months of working with Mann. This prejudice was a foreshadowing of that which he and other Baptist representatives faced when they attempted to occupy Lockwood House after the war. Much of the local community had objected to the use of the government building for a school for colored children, especially since a similar proposal had been rejected by town commissioners. Nonetheless, the Free Will Baptists persevered at Brackett's suggestion.

When the Harpers Ferry Mission School was officially instituted, the single building known as Lockwood House served as a dormitory, classrooms, and chapel. War refugees still remained in the basement and second-story level of the building until the Secondary Division of Storer College was instituted in 1867. The hall's second story was largely uninhabitable due to bombardment from Maryland Heights (located across the river) during the war. A German soldier, his wife, and child, however, occupied one room, until an undisclosed illness (perhaps complications from war wounds) finally took his life and his family left the house. The actual school activities of Lockwood House began in the southwest room of the first story, and afterward expanded to include the two adjoining south rooms in the front of the house. By 1869, the classroom and the school's chapel had been relocated to Anthony House and Lockwood House became primarily a dormitory. During the school year, it served as housing for male students, while in the summer it was operated as a hotel of sorts in order to bring in additional income for the fledgling college.

In 1878, in an effort to alleviate cramped living conditions at the college, Brackett planned a Mansard-style roof for Lockwood that would create additional space for ten rooms designated for female students. The aggressive project was ongoing, but it was not completed until 1883.

BRACKETT HOUSE

On July 27, 1865, a government "inspection report" claimed that the clerk's house, later Brackett House, was in "bad condition" after being abandoned by its former tenants, the United States Sanitary Commission (USSC). Nonetheless, the Brackett family moved into these quarters sometime between 1866 amd 1987. Despite its poor condition, Louise Brackett recalled that the former house of the superintendent's clerk was encircled with a fence "on line with the end of a flag stone walk," an addition that must have improved it aesthetically to some degree.

As the population of Camp Hill grew, the existing buildings strained to make room for the new residents. By March 1878, Brackett's correspondence suggested that Brackett House was reaching maximum capacity—not only physically but also psychologically. In a March 14, 1878, letter to Francis Mosher, founding member of the Missionary Society and the editor of denominational publications the *Myrtle* and the *Little Star*, Brackett indicated that "we have not felt that we could get along this way another year, i.e. be so crowded. We have but one sleeping room for our family of six and no room for hired girls." By publicizing the overcrowded conditions in the denomination's publications, Mosher used her media influence to help bring about the erection of Myrtle Hall at Storer College. The journalist also disseminated more generalized information about the college, making Brackett's needs in the valley known through the denomination's various publications. In spite of continued expansion of facilities, as late as 1880, twenty-three people still occupied the Brackett House. Principal Brackett, Louise Wood Brackett, his

Brackett House

wife; the four Brackett children, James W., Mary, Celeste E., and Ledru J.; Nathan Brackett's sister, Lura E.; three servants; and thirteen boarding female Storer students called Brackett House home. Mary Brackett (Robertson), the Bracketts' daughter, had an even stronger connection to the house than did her parents. She alleged in later years that "if family legend is correct, [I] was born in that house in November before the Act of Congress gave [it] to Storer College in December" in 1868.

MORRELL HOUSE

Morrell House began as the home of Benjamin Mills, who served as master armorer at the arsenal. Although a residence had been constructed for Mills in Lower Harpers Ferry, the armorer believed the location was unhealthy and, citing fear for his health, "refused to occupy the new house" along the town's flood plane. Accordingly, when in 1856 Armory Superintendent Clowe drafted plans for housing in Upper Harpers Ferry, the master armorer was included in the living arrangements. Until 1859 Mills would occupy what would become known as Morrell House.

In 1860, a minor controversy arose concerning the residence

Morrell House

when T. L. Patterson, Potomac Dam engineer, moved into the house. When word of Patterson's occupancy reached Colonel Craig, he immediately ordered then Superintendent Barbour to "remove" the engineer from the premises. Although Patterson did vacate the building, Colonel Craig's intention for the house's use—and thus the reason for his unusually harsh reaction—remain unknown.

Louise Wood Brackett wrote in a September 6, 1917, letter to Henry Temple McDonald, that Morrell House, by 1867, had become occupied by several "refugee families" trapped by the wake of confusion and generalized loss following the war. Although Morrell House was not deeded to the Free Will Baptists until December 15, 1869, Reverend Alexander Hatch Morrell had occupied it as early as 1867. After the Morrell family gained unofficial access to the house, the former paymaster's clerks' quarters possibly were enlarged, since Kate Anthony's 1891 "Historical Sketch" suggests that "additions" were made to the house. During the 1870 school term, Reverend Morrell and his wife shared the house with "twenty to twenty-seven girls," chaperoning and boarding them during the early crowded years. By 1880, census records indicated that joining Morrell in the house were his wife, Eliza [Seavy]; one daughter-in-law, Eliza J.; one grandchild, Joanna E.; and teacher Martha [W. L.] Smith.

It is fitting that one of the original buildings on campus became associated with the Morrell family name. The reverend had long worked tirelessly for the denomination. He had directed the Shenandoah Mission's religious activities, represented the Free Will Baptist-Home Mission Board, and eventually became the "soliciting agent" to generate funds and recruit students for Storer's programs. In fact, with the exception of a four-year period (1881–85), Morrell's adult life was devoted to serving the Free Will Baptist denomination on the campus of Storer College. A monolith with his mane is etched "Morrell" stands in the Curtis Memorial Chapel's courtyard as a tribute to his devotion.

ANTHONY HOUSE (MEMORIAL HALL)

In 1846, the government's appropriation for the United States Armory's superintendent's house, later to become Anthony Memorial Hall, amounted to $15,000, including $2,000 for the installation of a fresh-water cistern. Completed in July 1847, the house was a two-story brick dwelling with a "two-story wing connected by a passageway" to protect its inhabitants from the area's harsh weather. Key amenities—landscaping improvements, storage buildings, and fencing—were added to the superintendent's residence over time, in order to augment the real estate value of the federal property.

These improvements and protective enclosures made the superintendent's administrative residence a suitable overnight location for President Lincoln while he was at the federal installation on the evening of October 2, 1862. On that occasion, Lincoln had taken his private train car from Washington earlier in the day bound for Harpers Ferry. The president, under heavy guard, was on his way to visit Major General George B. McClellan. McClellan's army was then across the Potomac River in Sharpsburg, Maryland, recovering from the Battle of Antietam, which had been fought two weeks prior on September 17, 1862. Lincoln would soon relieve McClellan of his command for failing to pursue the Confederates in the wake of this bloody battle. Lincoln was increasingly frustrated by McClellan's disinclination to take decisive actions that might put the army at risk. After his dismissal, the former commander would continue to vex the president as the opposing Democratic nominee in the presidential election of 1864.

According to Mary Brackett (Robertson), even after the war's outcome her father was reluctant to relocate the fledgling school into Anthony Memorial Hall due to local opposition. Since pockets of resistance to the idea of a "colored school" still existed, Brackett wisely realized that attempts to develop further buildings other than the already-occupied Lockwood House could be seen as a provocation to local sensibilities. By keeping the Harpers Ferry Mission School's operation confined to Lockwood House, Brackett reasoned he would be better able to minimize oppositionist activities. The Free Will Baptists hoped that they

Anthony House

eventually could diffuse local opposition by proceeding with caution and extreme propriety. As a result, they did not feel at liberty to relocate the mission school and the school's chapel into Anthony

Memorial Hall until 1869. On December 23, 1869, the denomination dedicated the chapel in Anthony Memorial Hall, although this name would not become official for another decade.

In 1880 the denomination put plans to expand this former superintendent's quarters into operation. The need for expansion had become obvious by then. During the 1870s, the student population at Storer had increased considerably. This growth spurt meant that the Normal Department was repeatedly "hampered by its cramped condition" and other limitations. At the 1880 Centennial Conference, the Women's Missionary Society, with the assistance of Deacon Lewis Williams Anthony, began a "project to raise funds" in an attempt to alleviate the space constraints. They planned to renew the quarters to accommodate this crucial element of the school's operation. The women organized the project so that various denominational agencies "selected different rooms to finish and furbish."

In October 1871, Anthony had become a member of the Executive Committee of the Free Will Baptist-Home Mission Society, so he was well acquainted with the ongoing educational work at Storer College. Eight years later, in 1879, he was elected the society's president, which further spurred his interest in the Southern school. Anthony subsequently became a "liberal benefactor of the benevolent enterprises of the denomination," and he donated $5,000 of his own money for a multiple classroom addition to be built on the former superintendent's house.

Anthony Memorial Hall's original right wing, visible in the earliest pictures of Camp Hill, antedates the Civil War. The antebellum building had been used both as the private residence for the United States Armory's superintendent and later as a soldier's hospital after the war's onset. The denomination hired Washington, D.C., architect R. A. Gillis to design two 42.5-foot two-story square complementary annexes for each side of the existing forty-nine by ninety-eight-foot rectangular-shaped building to expand the hall via classroom wings. When completed, the annexes made the structure an imposing 130 feet in length. The cornerstones for the complementary annexes were laid on May 31, 1881, in conjunction with the fourteenth anniversary of the school. On the preceding day of this occassion, the noted orator and activist Frederick Douglass was invited from Washington, D.C., in addition to Andrew Hunter, the prosecutor of the John Brown Armory Raid trial.

Construction was completed the following year. The renovated structure was centered between the newly constructed boys' and girls' dormitories to the south and north, respectively. The main entrance was centered in the older section, while each of the annexes had separate entrances. Male students entered the building through the new eastern entrance in the southern annex, while female students entered through the eastern entrance in the original northern annex, the entrances closest to their respective dormitories.

Inside the new edifice, the "old chapel" was updated, refurbished, enlarged, and retained in the "left wing." The new complex also contained "a chapel, lecture rooms, recitation rooms, library, quarters for

Chapel and sometime classroom located in Anthony Hall

the principal's family, and janitor's rooms." For his dedication and generosity, Anthony received the honor of having the hall dedicated to him on May 30, 1882.

Anthony Memorial Hall developed into the focal point and primary activity center for the Storer College campus. With the four former government buildings now in use and named, respectively, for a wartime general and three dedicated churchmen—Lockwood, Brackett, Morrell, and Anthony—Storer College began the school's next developmental phase, the Secondary Division.

The school, however, continued to expand to accommodate the influx of secondary students while simultaneously offering preparatory classes to students in need of basic foundations in order to proceed to the next level of learning. To accommodate their students, the Board of Trustees approved plans to begin dormitory construction with aid from the Freedmen's Bureau.

Lincoln Hall

Consequently, the first major construction project on Storer's campus was Lincoln Hall, a dormitory for boys, named to honor "The Great Emancipator." With a $4,000 donation from the Freedmen's Bureau, between 1868 and 1870,

construction was completed on the "three story wooden building 40 x 75 feet containing 34 double rooms" just to the south of Anthony Memorial Hall. The dormitory had the capacity to board sixty-eight students, although during higher occupancy periods it is likely that these numbers were greater. Lincoln Hall was constructed by "a Union veteran" functioning as foreman of the "labor" force, which was made up of Storer's students enrolled for coursework during the period.

Old Lincoln Hall

Old Lincoln Hall school picture with Bracketts (center), Silas Curtis (left), and Reverend Morrell (right)

The idea for soliciting funds by touring one of the school's music ensembles was developed. In the summer of 1873, led by Anne Dudley and Martha Stowers, the Union Chorus (later to be known as The Harpers Ferry Singers) made their appeals on behalf of the school's needs while performing for various New York townships and cities from Buffalo to Utica. Not only did the group give *a capella* concerts to solicit donations from interested individuals, groups, and congregations, but ardent abolitionist minister Henry Ward Beecher at one point "yielded the pulpit of his church to Dudley for her entreaties." When the tour ended, it had raised $4,000, with an additional donation of $2,000 submitted by veteran abolitionist Gerrit Smith.

Myrtle Hall

Since space was always at a premium in the early days of Storer College, by the 1870s, the need for a girls' dormitory had become critical. In 1873, the foundation for such a dormitory was laid to the north of Anthony Memorial Hall, although the denomination— which maintained a particular aversion for the "dragging weight of debt"—did not initially have funds to complete the project. The building campaign was spearheaded by Frances Stewart Mosher, a denominational editor and an advocate of Storer who would later serve on the college's Boards of Instruction and Trustees.

Myrtle Hall

Western panoramic view: Lincoln Hall (left), Anthony Hall (center), Myrtle Hall (right)

With supplementary contributions toward construction costs by the Women's Missionary Society ($1,000) and the Centennial Jubilee Singers ($600), the project slowly came to fruition and finally, on May 30, 1876, the building was dedicated. Additionally, after reading about the building's further needs in the *Morning Star*, several New England churches, Sabbath schools, youth ministries, and other scholars sent offerings to completely finish the building. Individual gifts purchased "doors, windows, and even bricks" to complete the project for the next school term, when Myrtle Hall was opened. Unlike other campus buildings, the names of which derived from leaders and major contributors, the "Myrtle" of Myrtle Hall likely comes from the denomination's youth publication of the same name, perhaps a nod to the numerous children from northeastern churches who made its construction possible through their own penny-nickel-dime campaigns.

After the needed funds were raised, the cornerstone of the north-facing Myrtle Hall was laid five years later, in the summer of 1878. Two months later, Brackett reported that the first-floor elevation of the building was in place; in addition, other pertinent features of the building were well underway with "12 rooms on a floor [with each room] 12 x 16." Built upon a limestone base, the hall was constructed of brick, with an enhanced Mansard roof, a style that gave the building a spacious look. Dormer windows were installed into what was otherwise attic space. The brick dormitory featured ten windows abreast along its southern and northern exposures. The facade of the building was oriented east, echoing the same basic footprint as Anthony Hall.

It was reported to the Free Will Baptists that the new building later had a "one-story porch with [a] second story balustrade" opening to the outside. The balustrade's railing and banisters outlined the porch below. Upon its completion, Myrtle Hall housed the girls' preceptress and matron, boasted thirty-five rooms for students above the basement level, and provided in its basement a score of domestic operations, including cooking and laundry facilities.

During the 1880–81 school year, several improvements must have been made to Myrtle Hall. Miss Lura E. Brackett reported to the *Missionary Helper* in January that "in Myrtle hall we feel we are steadily gaining. The facilities for making the girls comfortable were much improved." The hall's completion and improvements extended over a long period of time, and despite their enthusiasm for the changes, the students, preceptress, and matron who lived there must have grown quite weary of the general inconvenience caused by ongoing construction. The women were pleased when the hall's improvements were finally completed, ending the clamor, the additional traffic caused by workmen, the increased noise level, and the disorder found amid supplies and materials littered throughout the hall. In winter 1881, all construction finally seems to have ceased, for Brackett stated that "for the first time we had the whole house to ourselves, undisturbed by plasterers, painters, etc."

During the 1881 school term, sixty women boarded in Myrtle Hall, with fewer than seven girls hiring outside assistance for "board and washing." In 1881, according to a report submitted by Lura Brackett, the Free Baptist Woman's Missionary Society was directly assisting fifty of those students, while ten others received indirect aid, although the type of assistance was not specified. The Free Baptist Woman's Missionary Society financed the hall's kitchen, study-room, and other projects, not only to improve the building, but also to support boarding students.

Before it was converted into a male dormitory in 1918, Myrtle Hall sustained two fires, one in 1883 and another in 1892. At some point between 1920 and 1930, Myrtle Hall was renamed Mosher Hall, as indicated on updates to the campus fire insurance schematic. After the building was renamed Mosher Hall, the building's first story was converted for use as a small physical education facility with "recreation and athletic rooms installed" for students, in addition to an infirmary room. The National Park Service finally demolished Myrtle Hall in 1963.

With four war-damaged buildings and two dormitories that were constructed over a period of years, the college campus was estalished.

Simultaneously, in order to meet the increasing demand for its services, it had to grow in focus, curricula, and scope. In addition to providing a foundational or basic education, Storer College evolved into an institution that, through its Secondary Division and [State] Normal Department, prepared others to take up the task of teaching.

Mosher Hall

Growth and Change

The Normal Department

Expansion of the elementary education offered by Storer did not occur without some concerted effort on the part of the college's creators. During the spring of 1867, the Free Will Baptists worked to open the Normal Department in time to qualify for assistance from the newly established Peabody Education Fund. Their efforts were fueled by the news that Barnas Sears, the fund's general agent, was planning a trip to select preexisting Southern schools that could qualify for funding. Sears was directed to select schools "in which the destitution [was] greatest and the number to be benefited largest" in order to quickly educate students for teaching in Southern schools. According to the "Circular of the General Agent of the Peabody Education Fund," which was widely disseminated throughout the South, the fund could not be used to found schools, assume routine support for or finance "literary" or "professional" schools. It was also not within the limits of the Peabody Education Fund to locate or hire teachers. To qualify, Storer's Normal Department had to be in place, organized, and functioning by the time Sears's arrived.

Oren B. Cheney wrote to Brackett that "in order to receive anything from the Peabody fund we must have a first class Normal School in operation" before Sears' arrival. Cheney reported to Brackett that "Dr. Sears will insist that we have a teacher who understands how to teach teaching." Thus, the Baptists began to look for a college graduate who had attended an approved "Normal School" for at least one term to begin the program.

Although the institutional planners were given a slight reprieve when Cheney discovered that Dr. Sears would not actually begin his southern tour until 1868, the college had already begun substantive work on its Normal Department. Together, the preparatory,

Anniversary exercises cover image

secondary, and normal departments would eventually offer the sort of education touted by the Free Will Baptists. This education combined traditional subjects meant to improve the mind with others meant to inculcate moral, ethical, and religious principles in the students.

The Storer Curriculum of Education and Morality

During the formative phase of Negro education, when institutions were first established for the sole purpose of educating freed and free blacks, Booker T. Washington claimed "the Negro worshiped books. We wanted books, more books. The larger the books were the better we like them. We thought the mere possession and the mere handling and the mere worship of books was going, in some inexplicable way, to make great and strong and useful men of our race." Washington's claim that the very concept of the book represented the potential for freedom and self-development indicates the level of desire inherent in those of his race for intellectual independence.

The Free Will Baptists' social and educational philosophies, which reflected their prevailing religious orthodoxy, made just such development possible. According to the canon of their religious faith, if adherents chose to live a life of elevated character, social tolerance, and moral integrity, their lives—by example—stimulated others to an improved lifestyle while simultaneously uplifting individuals and their society. Typical of the educational institutions of the period, Storer College directed its aims toward intellectual development combined with morality and Christian virtues. With these ends in view, school policy and practice included two Sabbath religious services and daily mandatory chapel attendance. As students from various religious backgrounds worshiped together, however, the mid-week prayer meetings were made optional. Regardless, the school emphasized the impossibility of intellectual enlightenment without moral development. Incorporated into Storer's "discipline" then was the principle that "teachers will spare no pains, both by precept and example, to inculcate good morals, habits of industry and self-dependence. It is, in fact, the design to make this a model school in every particular" for the common good. The school's educational foundation was based on the dedication of its founders to the principle of universal education, the diligent pursuit by its faculty of community-building, the institution of rules governing behavior, and the logical connection in its curriculum between "book-learning" and morality. Another noteworthy facet of Storer's educational experience was the selection of guest speakers whose own lives indicated the potential for success to Storer students.

In 1869, students had two different boarding options. They could either live in Lockwood House, or they could take rooms in privately owned houses with approved chaperones. If students chose to board in Lockwood, the room rent was $2 to $3. To offset this expense the Baptists "furnished [students] with employment to some extent" in order to defray the routine costs associated with formal schooling. However, boarding costs in private houses or cottages with "good families" cost $2 to $3 per week. The Baptists made exemptions for "indigent students," so that they too were offered opportunities for "habits of industry and self dependence."

During the 1882–84 session, Storer's students paid $2 to $5 for school books. Boarding dormitory students paid fifty cents for an "entrance fee" in order to defer upkeep and repairs for the "stove, double bedstead, table, and chairs" that furnished each dorm room. In 1882, students rented "beds complete"—$2 for three months, or $3 for eight months. If students preferred to furnish their own bedding, the school supplied clean straw for twenty cents per student.

The college charged students a weekly boarding fee of $1.50 to $1.75 paid "invariably in advance," an amount that came to a total of $6 to $7 per month. Tuition and room rentals were $1 to $1.50. Students could hire out their laundry for $1, while fuel costs ran between twenty-five to fifty cents per month. The total in expenses students could expect to pay per month ranged from $7.25 to $10, depending on their personal laundry habits and purchases of fuel for room heat. If students chose to board

themselves, their monthly expenses could benefit slightly by a $3 to $4 reduction. Students could purchase hot meals from local cooks for a nominal fee. Most cooks were colored women with families of their own, or enrolled children.

Throughout this period, Storer's founders did everything they could to make their education affordable—and to help those students who were not by themselves financially capable of attending. Although its founders were especially concerned with maintaining adequate

Schoolwide assembly on the hillside slope outside New Lincoln (later Brackett) Hall

funding during Storer's formative years, when the need to improve facilities ran high, they were also aware that most, if not all, of their students could hardly afford to attend (and benefit) without some sort of assistance. Their clientele demanded that they make allowances—literally.

STORER'S FINANCIAL DEDICATION TO EDUCATION

The Free Will Baptists designed their Southern school so that "expenses were reduced as low as possible," so that none would be excluded or "debarred from the privileges of study" due to lack of financial means. To help finance their education, many of Storer's "first students were given work on the grounds and in repairing the old buildings and in cultivating the farm," tending its gardens, crops, and livestock.

As is the case today, the cost of an education during the nineteenth century could be prohibitive. In 1869, the general tuition range at Storer was between $3 and $9, depending upon whether students enrolled per term ($3), or for the full year ($9). If students "guaranteed five years of instruction," they purchased a "Certificate of Scholarship" from the school's treasurer for $20. As is the case at most universities today, the school charged an additional fee for students enrolled in special courses—"Drawing, Painting and Instrumental Music"—that would be used to cover costs for specialized utensils, equipment, and instrument rentals.

Storer's Faculty

In order to ensure that the college did indeed meet this overriding goal, the denomination looked first to its faculty. To begin with, the school's creators sought an integrated team of teachers. When the school opened its doors in 1867, its first nineteen students were under the charge of Miss Martha Smith, who began her career as a teacher working with "contrabands" near Hampton, Virginia, during General Butler's command of Fortress Monroe. For the full 1867–68 school term, however, the Free Will Baptist Home Mission Society approved thirteen teachers to be sent to the Shenandoah Valley and the Storer campus. Additionally, during the term, Brackett and Morrell also employed "seven colored assistant missionaries" to work alongside the new cohort. The employment of these seven tallied with the society's desire to eventually replace Northern workers with "colored students" who had been educated at Storer College. These students would be prepared "to become teachers and preachers" who would continue to generate "support [from] the people residing there" long after the Northern workers returned to their places of origin.

In addition, the denomination believed the responsibilities of its teachers should extend beyond classroom education into the local community and moral and social spheres. With the passage of time and growing community needs, the mission teachers' responsibilities were thus expanded. They were expected to work toward the betterment of their communities. For example, Anne Dudley, assisted by Miss E. H. Oliver (another mission teacher), organized the first Free Will Baptist church in Martinsburg in Berkeley County. The two women were "assisted by a colored preacher," who aided them and solicited others to help on their behalf. Shortly thereafter, other churches were organized in Harpers Ferry and in Charles Town. Consequently, "the work of the mission [was] perpetuated in the churches" by like-minded individuals—black and white—who believed in the mission's attempt to morally and educationally improve the quality of life for valley residents. Through the examples set by its teachers, Storer enabled its students and the community to realize that "good moral character" was important for everyday living. Additionally, it created a set of rules and regulations—set forth in each year's catalogue—which helped define its students' moral characters.

Storer's Rules of Conduct

Increasing enrollment prompted Storer's administration to enact more specific rules governing conduct and behavior. The administration openly stated that its students were "presumed to be ladies and gentlemen" and, as such, they were welcome to take advantage of college offerings "only so long as the presumption is maintained." To remind students about this presumption, the college administration provided them with a "strict code of conduct, carefully laid out in each year's catalogue." These definitive "requirements and prohibitions" were so clearly defined as to allow no misinterpretation.

In order to remain enrolled, students were directed to adhere to "all the regulations for the promotion of health, cleanliness and good order" on behalf of the school. Storer's regulations also were designed to help students succeed academically. Attendance for "recitation" and other extracurricular "exercise" was mandatory for all students unless excused for good reason by a member of the faculty. When the school's study bell rang, students were expected to immediately report to their rooms to observe quiet study hours until last call for lights-out.

Additionally, students were expected to prepare for each day's classes with a one-hour study session before the school day started. Students were not allowed to add or drop classes, or transfer from one class to another for any reason. To deter distracting or casual assemblies, students were not allowed to "loiter" about the campus, so that students attending classes or participating in study sessions were not disturbed.

In order to complete the totality of its mission, however, Storer's prohibitions extended beyond the educational needs to the social lives of its students. For obvious reasons, students were not allowed to leave campus without permission, particularly to "attend balls, dances or other parties in the town"—and such permission was never an option during the school week. Social outings were generally discouraged, especially "pleasure excursions, rides, or walks, in mixed company," unless the group was accompanied by faculty, or given special permission. As might seem logical for a church-affiliated school, the rules specifically prohibited students from visiting "any drinking saloon," imbibing "intoxicating liquors," and using "profane or indecent language" that would reflect negatively on the student population or the school. Over the years the prohibition of "intoxicating liquors" became a recurrent (but minor) problem, especially in cases where Storer's football team traveled into the District of Columbia to play Howard University. The Storer-Howard game evolved into quite a regional rivalry.

Students also were not allowed to "play cards, jump, dance or scuffle" in buildings, or to smoke in or near "the grounds of the Institution, or on the streets." Students were not allowed "to have or use fire-arms," except with special permission from the school's principal. Since students were allowed to live off-campus, they could board only in approved boardinghouses with approved chaperones. They could not relocate without special permission, and they were discouraged against indebtedness of any kind.

As might also be expected, rules governed interaction between the sexes. While some such rules seemed to focus more narrowly on

decreasing the potential for sexual activity—by no means were students allowed to invite "persons of the opposite sex" to their rooms—others seemed geared more toward protecting the "fairer sex" in general. For example, female students "were not allowed to be out after dark," could not be seen alone in the company of a man, and were not even permitted to go to the railroad station without a chaperone to escort them to and from the school's campus.

In addition to these rules, a comprehensive dress code was instituted for students. Realizing that "a decided movement toward reformation in the dress of school girls" was coming into fashion, the school

Football practice formation by the 1909 Golden Tornadoes

was just as determined "to establish a standard" to avoid controversy. Female students were advised to keep their dress "simple" with no jewelry, no "silk or velvet," no "ornaments" of any kind. The catalogue clearly states that "from the teacher's point of view, the schoolroom is a workshop, not a place for cast-off finery . . . the best and most economical material for school dresses is mohair alpaca." Mothers were asked to provide daughters with "a plaited woolen shirt attached to a lining waist, and an elastic Jersey bodice . . . with one undershirt and two layers of underclothing—one pure wool, the other cotton . . . and a corded corset waist, to which the stocking suspenders are attached [which] neatly outlines; without compressing, the figure."

Admission Standards to the General Curriculum

The nature of Storer College's admission standard indicated the school's philosophy that education and morality did not have to be mutually exclusive. In 1869 and for several years thereafter, admission required first that students "give satisfactory evidence of a good moral character." In addition, students had to demonstrate proficiency in reading, spelling, penmanship, geography, and mental arithmetic before they could be enrolled in the "Regular Course of Study." According to the school's educational philosophy, "the greater the proficiency the student has made in these branches, the better will he be able to master the studies of the Course." If students were unable to demonstrate proficiencies in each area, they were enrolled in the "Preparatory

Department" instead of the "Regular Course of Study" at Storer. Once students were enrolled in the "Regular Course," they were expected to complete the gradated course over a three-year period.

The college offered three terms for students. The fall term included the months of September through December. January through the month of March made up the winter term, and the summer term was extended through the months of April to June. This trimester system remained in effect until the late 1870s, when it was changed to a "regular session." The "regular session" began the first week of October and culminated on Memorial Day, although students did have one week off for Christmas vacation and another "few days the last of March."

During the nineteenth century, it was common for courses of study to be offered in what sounds to us like reverse chronology. First-year students entered the "Third Year," or the least difficult curriculum, and over the course of time worked their way up to the "First Year," or most difficult curriculum. Storer's curriculum followed this tradition. Students entering the first year of study, the "Third Year," were expected to advance through fundamental work in "Reading" from third- and fourth-grade primers, "Spelling," the beginning level of "Intermediate Geography," and "Elementary Arithmetic," coupled with "First Lessons in Grammar, Penmanship, Recitations and Compositions." To these subjects, "Second Year" students added reading in fourth- and fifth-grade primers, a complete "Geography" course, "Common School Arithmetic," and "Common School Grammar and

Analysis." The "Second Year" curriculum also introduced a course on the "History of the United States."

Culminating the three-year program of study, the "First Year" class focused on more advanced subjects such as "Algebra, Physiology, Moral Science, and Natural Philosophy." "First Year" students were also expected to write "Original Declamations and Compositions," as well as take a methods course, "Instruction in the Art of Teaching" to complete the normal program. This last course was mandatory and funding from the Peabody Education Fund required it.

By 1875, the growth of the college was rapid and the "aggregate number of pupils . . . was 285" at Storer College. The entry year by that time was reclassified as the "First Year" instead of the "Third Year," and the school adhered to a strict, forward chronology from this point corresponding with the number of years individual students were in attendance at the institution.

Even during these early years, the traditional classroom experience was often rounded out by a series of in-house and guest lectures designed to broaden students' awareness of the world around them and their places within it. The guest lectures at the college were to become an important part of the ongoing legacy of Storer.

Storer's Lecture Series

In order to prove a well-rounded education consistent with Victorian influences, the creators of Storer College believed students should be challenged by the experiences of others and exposed to various ideas through those experiences. In keeping with this principle, the school's 1880s catalogues claimed that "to listen to great orators is a most important part of a student's education." Every day, at the close of recitations, students were given a "talk or select reading" for fifteen minutes. Lectures addressed a number of subjects, such as "School Discipline, Political Economy, Morals, Physiology, History, [and] the events of the day." Complementing this lecture period, students were encouraged to participate by posing questions, offering comments, opinions, and "minute speeches" making further application of their learning process through inquisition and interaction.

In addition, as noted in the 1876 "Resources of West Virginia," the school boasted "an annual course of lectures on scientific, and other topics," which the compilers of the report believed to be "an excellent feature in its administration." More importantly, however, at various times, the slate of in-house lectures was expanded by guest lectures provided by some of the most influential speakers of the day. On May 30, 1881, for example, the occasion of Storer's fourteenth anniversary, Frederick Douglass delivered a commencement address on the legacy proffered by the actions of John Brown. Douglass's presence served to remind the students that education provided the ultimate escape from the bonds of slavery. He wrote that slave owners had viewed illiteracy and ignorance as weapons, as powerful as the whip and branding iron for ensuring enslavement. Douglass proclaimed education as "the pathway from slavery to freedom," which he personally exemplified. In one situation, as Douglass recounts, his mistress began to teach him to read, but his master, who warned his wife that her efforts would "spoil" the young slave, halted the plan.

Douglass stated, "I now understood what had been to me a most perplexing difficulty—to wit, the white man's power to enslave the black man. From that moment, I understood the pathway from slavery to freedom." His awareness fueled his ardor for educating his fellow blacks, as his commencement address indicates. That Douglass could publicly praise John Brown as a heroic crusader for the end of slavery on a speaker's rostrum in Harpers Ferry perhaps illustrates that great progress that had been made toward the assimilation of freedmen since the war years. Once Douglass had been forced to break the law to teach fellow slaves, but to the students at Storer he could speak freely about the potential for advancement offered by education. Much had changed over the course of the last thirty years—and many more changes were yet to come.

Frederick Douglass

Key Changes During the First Phase of Storer's Existence

As the world around Storer continued to change, the school likewise adapted and evolved on a number of levels, from the size of its teaching staff to its rules for students, from its curriculum to its educational scope. In 1869, the "Board of Instructors" was comprised of seven instructors and three examiners. Brackett remained the principal while his wife, Louise, was "Teacher of Drawing and Painting." Miss Martha J. Stowers was the acting "Preceptress" and "Teacher of Music," assisted by Miss Dora J. Stockbridge. The "Lecturers" consigned to the "Board of Instructors" were Calder, Ball, and Brewster from the instituting commission board. The Rev. G. G. Baker, E. S. Lacy, and J. T. Furgerson served as the school's early "Examining Committee" for students.

By 1882, Storer College had expanded its Board of Instructors to accommodate a more diversified curriculum. Principal Brackett was teaching "Arithmetic and Political Economy" and Louise Wood

Class of 1893, Academic Department

Another important change involving the teaching staff occurred during the early 1880s. For the first time, the official Board of Instructors included African American full-time instructors. Miss Coralie Lee (Cook) Franklin, an 1880 Storer graduate, became the teacher of "elocution," instructing students in the arts of public reading and speaking. Likewise, William Henry Bell served as a general "Assistant and Steward" to the faculty at Storer. Born a slave in Fairfax County, Virginia, in 1839, Bell had served as a soldier for the Union Army during the Civil War. With his interesting background— first a slave and then a fighter for freedom—Bell most likely provided the Storer College students of the 1880s with a unique perspective on the most important historical move-

Brackett, was reassigned as assistant principal. One of Brackett's younger sisters, Lura Ellen Brackett, taught "English Grammar and Algebra," and during the period 1882–1884 served as preceptress. Eventually, students expressed a great affinity for the strictly structured, Victorian woman they began to refer to as "Miss Lue," and she devoted the best years of her life to them, remaining at Harpers Ferry until her death in 1925.

ments of the century. Franklin and Bell were joined by Mrs. D. B. Washington, who taught "Instrumental Music." Laura Taylor, Lizzie Simms, John B. Spriggs, and Bernard Tyrrell were "Assistant Pupils," selected from among the student population to aid their teachers while gaining experience at the same time from faculty mentors.

Rev. D. Waterman.

Other supporting faculty in the early 1880s included the Reverend Dexter Waterman, an ordained minister who was responsible for teaching "Scripture History and Butler's Theology." Additionally, Waterman functioned as a mentor for male students interested in becoming preachers. When he was a member of the Board of Instructors at Storer, he was nearly eightly years old but was still an active minister, preaching each Sunday. He also served as a member of Storer's Board of Trustees. Walter Paul Curtis of Auburn, Maine, the nephew of school founder Silas Curtis, provided instruction in "Latin and Natural Sciences."

During this period, the Board of Instructors also maintained several rotating "Assistants" who alternated working with full-time and part-time faculty. Based on the "Biennial Catalogue of the Officers and Students of Storer College, Academic and State Normal Departments, 1882–1884,"

among those who served in this capacity for the school were C. A. E. Southwell, Mrs. E. C. Jenness, and W. D. Wilson and J. P. Lovett, who had graduated with elocution teacher Franklin. At times, musical education was handled by Mrs. M. R. Adams, who was responsible for vocal music, and Mrs. D. B. Washington, who taught instrumental music. In 1882, the "Matron" of Myrtle Hall, the girl's dormitory, was identified as Miss Emily Carter.

The McDonalds pose alongside the bandmaster with one of the school's noted female instrumental bands

Growth and Change

By the 1880s, the curriculum also had undergone considerable changes, primarily to accommodate the needs of what had become three distinct departments: Preparatory, Academic and State Normal. In the 1882–1884 term, 166 students were enrolled in the school's Preparatory Department, which was itself divided into "Grade A" and "Grade B" classes. During this period, there were 92 students in "Grade A" and 74 students in "Grade B." At the same time, the Academic Department had enrolled 59 students with the express intention of preparing to "fit students for the first-class colleges" over a course of four years. Listed in the 1882–1884 Biennial Catalogue as a member of the Academic Department's "First Class" is Mary Brackett [Newcomer], the youngest child of Nathan and Louise. Mary was eventually sent to New England to complete her education because the school had not achieved collegiate status—but she began her education alongside the children, and grandchildren of freedmen and free blacks at Storer, in keeping with the inclusive principles of the Free Will Baptists.

Of the three departments, the Academic one recorded the smallest enrollment, yet from its conception "it represented the core of what Storer's founders and administration hoped the school would become— a respected college for African Americans that could offer courses of the caliber of a traditional liberal arts education." Its curricula focused on the classics, such as Ovid, Cicero, and Virgil. English literature was another area of study, including Shakespeare, along with Latin and Greek grammar. Foreign languages, such as German and French also

were taught, as well as a variety of traditional high school level subjects, including algebra, geology, botany, and astronomy.

The school's State Normal Department provided the most academically advanced education. Sixty-three students were enrolled for the three-year program of normal school training during the 1882–1884 academic school year. During this period, the suggested curriculum increased by number and in difficulty from six courses in the "First Year" to eleven for the "Third Year" students preparing for graduation. Storer's "Board of Instructors" and Principal Brackett worked with the West Virginia State superintendent of schools to design the Normal Course, so that students upon graduation were qualified "to teach in this and adjoining States" with certificates of proof.

After 1870, the West Virginia State superintendent of schools was automatically allocated an *ex officio* position with the school's four-member Board of Trustees. The school relied on these officials for up-to-date information and regulatory recommendations. The trustees believed the program's success was due in part to the amount of reading exercises and activities "from which no student [was] excused." Students were exposed to the "useful arts" as well. For example, female students were given instruction in "needle-work" while male students were taught to a more limited degree the art, design, and techniques of printing. Although the school did have a "Biblical Class," it was not referred to as a department per se. The "Biblical Class" was designed to provide "some knowledge of [Biblical] history and geography," including the "fundamental doctrines of the Scriptures," especially for students interested in preaching. Discussions in the "Biblical Class" were perhaps invigorated by the fact that they often contained representatives of diverse religious sects and backgrounds simultaneously.

During the 1880s, a period that marks the close of the first phase of Storer's development, another noteworthy change occurred. Whereas in preceding years the school catalogue indicated that students were admitted without distinction on account of "color, or race," they now began to be admitted "without distinction on account of race, sex, or religious preference." Students from fourteen different states attended classes in Harpers Ferry from as far away as Illinois in the west, Maine in the north, Georgia in the south, and Maryland along the east coast. The school's reach also expanded beyond the borders of the United States. The second phase of Storer's existence witnessed the arrival of students from Canada, Liberia, Bermuda, and Port Republic. One such student, Hamilton H. Hatter, of Buxton, Ontario, graduated from the Academic Department in 1884. He then completed his formal education at Bates College and returned to West Virginia "as an instructor in the Sciences and Languages at Storer College" before being elected principal of Bluefield Colored Institute by the West Virginia Board of Regents.

As Hatter built the school at Bluefield, he turned to Storer graduates for assistance. Thanks to the influence of Hatter, Nathan Wood Brackett served as the president of the school's Board of Regents. Hatter's efforts—and his dedication to the region—exemplifies the influence of Storer College both nationally and internationally. By 1883, the list of foreign students at Storer had grown to include four students from Africa.

By 1884, records indicate that some four hundred teachers in West Virginia, Maryland, Virginia, Ohio, and Pennsylvania had attended the college for "at least some time," while 112 students had formally graduated from the Normal Department. Storer was the "only school above primary grade" available for students within a three-hundred-mile radius for a considerable period of time. As the decade drew to a close, a denominational publication, *The Free Baptist Cyclopedia—Historical and Biographical*, indicated "the number of teachers trained at Storer had grown to nearly 500." Truly, by the end of this important second phase of its development, Storer College had not only met most of its initial goals but also had begun to expand its mission. The stage was set for further secondary expansion in the years from 1884–1921, when the Industrial, Biblical, and Musical departments were developed and the school struggled for financial security.

Rose Johnson, Class of 1900

Growth and Change

Secondary Expansion, 1884–1921

The next phase of Storer College's expansion included realignment of the school's mission to include industrial, musical and biblical education. There were a number of obstacles that seemed destined to limit that potential, however, including a decrease in financial assistance from and crises within the Free Will Baptist denomination. During the same period, the school also witnessed its first major administrative change. As the nineteenth century faded into the twentieth, Storer struggled to maintain its original course and expand to meet the demands of the nation's growing need for industrial workers.

The Campus

At the end of the nineteenth century, most of the elements that characterized the growth of Storer in its early years remained constant. The school remained dedicated to helping students financially and, through a continuing series of lectures, educationally. Most importantly, the State Normal Department continued its record of preparing teachers to carry on the business of educating others.

The original campus buildings on Camp Hill were a sign of continuity, altered slightly over time to meet the growing needs of residents and students. While other construction projects elsewhere on campus would be undertaken during this phase of Storer's existence, one very important structure from its past remained a viable element of its present. Lockwood House, the school's original home, was in disrepair

An aerial view of the campus of Storer College

when Brackett and others took up residence there in the late 1860s, but the years saw a number of improvements. By 1894 two more outer buildings had been annexed to Lockwood House to extend its footage, according to schematic diagrams drawn that year. Also, between 1902 and 1907, its western portico was extended northward to wrap around the structure toward what was known as Fillmore Avenue.

Always important to Storer's history, Lockwood House also became an important fixture in the community. In 1900 it opened year-round to boarders. The Lovetts, Sarah and William, a mulatto family, managed the boarding operation with a fleet of "cooks, waitresses, chambermaids, [a] business manager, mail carriers and gardeners," incorporating a variety of "entertainments" for their boarders. After the Lovetts gave up management, their middle child, Maggie Lovett Daniels, and her husband Allen took over and were still operating the house in 1923, when Henry Temple McDonald notified them that the college intended to enact its right of possession by September 1, 1924.

Financial and Educational Assistance for Students

The school provided financial assistance when possible to poor students during these years of growth and change. With a philosophical grounding in the concept of student self-management and independence, the school had assisted students who lacked sufficient funds with on-campus opportunities to defray the cost of tuition and board. The *Storer Record* supported this program, indicating its endorsement

by arguing that students "benefited much more by having a chance to earn the money" instead of having it given to them or owing it. During this period, students could earn toward tuition and board by "cleaning up rooms, . . . cultivating a garden, . . . mending furniture for the school, or . . . teaching a small preparatory class" to first-year students. The industrious student could also find off-campus work.

In addition, during this period the state of West Virginia began to lend its support to the financial aid effort. In due course, based upon its desire to staff the numerous Negro schools that sprang up within its borders, the state also approved educational scholarships—including "free tuition, room-rent and use of books"—as incentives for students who wished to enter the Normal Department. For the 1897 school term, the sixty-three students enrolled in the college's teacher training program received free textbooks and tuition. By 1921, more than ten other scholarships and awards became available to students.

Students also had an opportunity to win several academic prizes. There were three higher educational institutions that offered awards. Howard and Lincoln universities, and Bates College in Lewiston, Maine, all had competitive awards available to Storer students. There was an "Alumni Award" for one male and one female. A "Brewster Award" was given to one person in each of the freshman, sophomore, and junior classes. The Metcalf Scholarship was offered to one each of the four different classes. Students were encouraged to apply for the

Anthony W. Lewis and Ida Stillman scholarships. The Anthony Memorial Scholarship and the Archibald Johnson Honor Medal were given to the senior student with the highest score.

Students continued to benefit from hearing a number of guest lecturers who routinely visited the campus. Visiting ministers provided numerous lectures. For example, Reverend Earnest G. Wesley of Providence, Rhode Island, was on campus to "deliver a course of lectures" during spring 1895. A well-traveled and an accomplished author and musician, Wesley focused his lecture series on seven subjects: "Teaching, Romanism, Deity of Christ, Social Purity, Missions, Personal Work, [and the] Bible." In keeping with the Free Will Baptists' early 1800s "universal" perspective, the Baptists initiated a practice of inviting various ministers, preachers, and other religious representatives to address the student body's Sunday congregations at the Curtis Memorial Church. Women were sometimes featured as the speakers, an unusually progressive feature.

Curtis Memorial Chapel, 1892

The Baptists' early interdenominational outlook was maintained as both the denomination and its administration sought to provide a rich, well-balanced educational context for students. Educators and other professionals also spoke to students. Frances Mosher, a visiting professor from Hillsdale College before accepting a permanent position at Storer, came to the campus in February 1895 as she returned from a Woman's Council Meeting in Washington, D.C. According to the *Storer Record*, Mosher "gave an interesting talk to the general history class on Martin Luther" and a "most enjoyable lecture before the Woman's League to which the public was invited." Students learned about the art of "Success" from Tracy L. Jeffords, an attorney then practicing in Washington, D.C.

A meteorological lecture was given by another guest lecturer, John R. Weeks, from Binghampton, New York, entitled "The Weather, What It

Is and How It Is Forecast." Dr. Robert W. Douthat from Morgantown, West Virginia, visited the campus in 1907 and 1908 to present a lecture on the "The Battle of Gettysburg" and an overview of "God in History." The history of the Civil War was also the focus when Major L. P. Williams detailed the deplorable war time conditions of Libbey Prison.

Thomas E. Robertson discussed scientific advancements through "Wireless Telegraphy" with students. J. R. Wilder's address was directed toward "The Race Problem." In 1904, E. O. Taylor scientifically approached the "Origin and Effects of Alcohol" on campus.

A noted opponent of "Jim Crow" laws, Mary Church Terrell likely captured the student body's attention with her address entitled "The Bright Side of a Dark Subject" in 1907. Terrell was an educator, fluent in several languages, and the first woman of color to serve on the District of Columbia's school board. On July 14, 1896, Terrell had attended a national conference to form the National Association of Colored Women (later, Women's Clubs). Terrell, along with Ida B. Wells-Barnett and others, organized this group, which became one of the most powerful African American women's organizations in the United States. This occurred after they were discriminated against at the Columbian Exposition of 1893 in Chicago.

Also in 1907, George Wesley Atkinson, an ex-governor of West Virginia, addressed the student body on "'The Integrity of the College Student." Nathan Wood Brackett and Atkinson had developed a long-standing social and political relationship during the 1880s, when

Mary Church Terrell

Atkinson chaired the Republican Party in West Virginia before his gubernatorial bid.

In addition, visiting friends of current faculty members often took the opportunity to address students on a variety of entertaining and enlightening topics, from music to travel. Visiting her friend Mary Brackett, for example, Maine resident Dora Jordan "gave the school a very enjoyable talk on her trip [to] Scotland." This diverse slate of lecturers further demonstrates the administration's expectation that students would be provided with as much exposure as possible to other perspectives, opinions, and places in the world during their time on campus.

Eventually the administration not only welcomed guest lecturers but also began to incorporate music recitals and ensemble performances. In 1908, Storer's students were exposed to the talents of two vocalists, one from New England and the other from the Midwest: Nellie

Growth and Change

Brown Mitchell from Roxbury, Massachusetts, and Anita Brown, a resident of Chicago, Illinois. The "DeKoven Male Quartette" and the "College Girls Quartette" also gave concerts that same year. Throughout the period, as the state's growing endorsement of it indicates, the college's State Normal Department, long applauded for its successful training methods, remained one of the most successful elements in Storer's evolution.

The Second Niagara Conference

In 1906, Storer's campus became the site for a very significant historical event. In that year, the college hosted the first American conference of the Niagara Movement, the antecedent organization for the National Association for the Advancement of Colored People (NAACP). The organization had met for the first time the preceding year, in 1905, on the Canadian side of Niagara Falls, since no lodging was open to them on the American side. "J. R." Clifford, a local attorney and an 1875 graduate of Storer College, operated as W. E. B. Du Bois's local liaison to coordinate the details of the national meeting. Since "coloreds" during the period were unable to find mass lodging to accommodate such a sizable gathering, the delegates likely stayed on campus in Old Lincoln Hall, just south of Anthony Hall.

At the national meeting, Du Bois launched an appeal for the right to vote; an end to discrimination in public accommodations; the "right to walk, talk, and be with them that wish to be with us

Second Niagara Conference (1906) founding father W. E. B. Du Bois is seated. Standing are (left to right) John Robert "J. R." Clifford (West Virginia's first African American attorney), L. M. Henshaw, and F. H. M. Murray.

[without] interference," and for the "federal government to step in and wipe out illiteracy," later called "the Credo." The substance of Du Bois's Niagara Movement Speech, addressed to a national public assembly, served not only as the nucleus for Du Bois's lifelong project but also as his oppositionist rebuttal to Booker T. Washington's appeal for accommodation and assimilation. Three years later, in 1909, the NAACP was officially organized to prevent racially motivated violence and deter discriminatory practices. In August, 2009, Storer would celebrate its Centennial Anniversary on the campus, with national officers, delegates, and dignitaries in attendance."

Second Niagara Conference auxiliary members: Mrs. Gertrude Wright Morgan (seated) and (left to right) Mrs. O. M. Waller, Mrs. H. F. M. Murray, Mrs. Mollie Lewis Kelan, Mrs. Ida D. Bailey, Miss Sadie Shorter, and Mrs. Charlotte Hershaw

Three years later, in 1909, the NAACP was officially organized to prevent racially motivated violence and deter discriminatory-based practices. And, in 2009, the Niagara Movement will celebrate its Centennial Anniversary again on the campus of Storer College, in August, with national officers, delegates and dignitaries in attendance.

STORER'S EDUCATION OF TEACHERS CONTINUES

The school's administration was decidedly in favor of enlightening its student population by any means available, and most especially its normal students. By 1895, twenty-seven years after its inception, Storer's Normal Department had produced hundreds of teachers. As the *Storer*

Record indicated that year, the school's education program, although its entry classes were small, "was among the first in the South to send out competent teachers of the "colored" race." The first class of the department numbered only eight, but by 1895 the department graduated 250, "nearly all of whom have become leaders among their people" in their "colored" communities. The performance of Storer graduates on state teacher examinations and the sheer number of those who were gainfully employed in the profession across West Virginia and other states indicate the struggle had paid off.

Storer graduates did quite well on state teacher examinations, which could be difficult. Annually, students—either graduates, or near graduates—from West Virginia's normal schools were examined by counties to which they were making application for future employment. County examiners, including the local superintendents of schools, were brought together to form three-member Examination Committees. There were three grades of evaluation. Those teacher applicants maintaining a 90 percent average for each phase of testing with no grades falling below 75 percent were awarded a "Grade No. 1." Those applicants with an 80 percent average, with no score below 65 percent, received a "Grade No. 2" marking. Applicants with a 70 percent average, with no score below 60 percent, were given a "Grade No. 3." If applicants achieved the "Grade No. 1" evaluation, they were thereafter reexamined only on subjects for which they received a grade below 82 percent. In order to maintain not only their initial grade status but also for purposes of certification renewal, normal teachers were assessed on "two additional studies" annually. The "two additional studies" were probably unidentified—a tactic sure to function as preparation stimulus.

Mary Franklin Clifford, an 1872 graduate

In 1895, the *Storer Record* reported on one such county teacher examination. During the public examinations, which were held at some point between 1890 and 1895, Storer sent sixteen teacher applicants to an unidentified county in West Virginia. Most applicants had completed the normal training, but the faculty encouraged a few normal candidates just nearing completion to proceed with the exam. The Storer students arranged to take the examination along with double the number of white teachers. The Storer students' papers were "examined and marked" accordingly in each "branch" by the County Examination Committee, all of whom had been selected by local authorities. The students from Storer's Normal Department performed well on the examination. In fact, the collective percentage earned by the Storer students averaged a "little higher than [that of] the white teachers." This is indicative of Storer's success since "there was a white Normal School in the same county" from which most of the students taking the exam had graduated, and from which members of the examination committee also likely graduated.

The success of Storer's students on such examinations was possibly attributable to a new mandatory requirement that students academically engage with instructors in a more intimate setting and on a more complicated intellectual plane. During the 1890s, the college instituted a new academic standard for advanced students at Storer. The "Academic and Senior Normal students" began to meet with faculty members on a weekly basis in order "to read and discuss literary works." This was an atmosphere in which the open exchange of ideas was not only encouraged but expected. For example, during the 1898–1899 term, authors whose works were slated for discussion with faculty included: Burke, Webster, Lowell, Longfellow, Irving, Wordsworth, Eliot, Whittier, and Shakespeare. The open-forum prerequisite for advanced "Academic and Senior Normal" students, coupled with the mandatory "Peabody Teacher Institute" that was established on campus sometime between 1870 and 1882, served to raise the school's educational standards.

In this manner, the "Academic and Senior Normal" regimen likely elevated students' sense of self-confidence and mental acumen for examining differing perspectives on issues. Such open-forum opportunities for students would later suitably correspond with the administration's plans to offer advanced pedagogical, managerial, psychological, sociological, economical, ethical, and legal coursework. This was in the interest of junior college accreditation for the school and certified endorsement for its graduates.

In 1895, the *Storer Record* declared that the twenty operating "free schools" in Jefferson County, West Virginia, were "taught by former students" of the institution. The college's students were also working in other "important schools all over the state." Peyton H. Callaway graduated from the Normal Department in 1891 and in 1896 taught in Powellton, West Virginia, before going on to earn his doctorate. In 1896, Mary Hawkins was teaching at a private school in Winchester, Virginia. At Salem, Virginia, Mollie Hughes was simultaneously teaching for both the school system and a local church, walking five miles each week to take charge of a Sunday School class. Robert E. Lee, from McGaheysville, Virginia, graduated from the Academic Department in 1889, then attended medical school at the Western University of Pennsylvania, graduating in 1896. George Green and John Veney, listed as members of the Normal Department's third class (1869), were fondly recalled as some of Storer's "early students" and warmly received by the campus for a denominational meeting in later years.

By 1900, graduates of the Normal Department were scattered across the nation, from Maryland in the northeast to Texas in the southwest. Several other graduates, according to the *Storer Record*, had begun work at "higher institutions" to correspond with study programs begun on Storer's campus. In 1895, it was noted that one of the school's graduates was appointed "Preceptress" at the Princess Ann Branch of Morgan College in Maryland. Two others were full professors at the Virginia Seminary located in Lynchburg, Virginia, a feeder-school for Virginia Union. Another student became a "Professor of Mathematics" in the Virginia English and Classical Institute at Petersburg, Virginia. The teachers of music and domestic science at the West Virginia Colored Institute in Kanawha County, West Virginia, (the second Negro college to be established in the state after Storer), were graduates of Storer College. In keeping with the humanitarian spirit with which Storer was established, the "Matron" and "Assistant Matron" at the National Home for Colored Orphans in Washington, D.C., were also graduates of the school at Harpers Ferry.

During the 1880s the basic departmental divisions at Storer College remained intact, with the Normal Department receiving the greatest amount of publicity for its educational endeavors. However, the last two decades of the century also witnessed a number of changes, from additions to the physical campus, to a change in administration, to the development of new departments (including one that was embroiled in controversy).

Growth and Change

New Buildings, New Administration, and New Departments

As with any institution, the progress of time inevitably is accompanied by alterations in makeup, courses, and style. Storer College is no exception. In the developmental phase of the college, which lasted from from 1884 to 1921, it had matured sufficiently to assert its own need to grow, to usher in a new administrator, and to respond to the nation's growing need for industrial workers.

The first few years of Storer's existence were marked by its creators' attempts to wrest space from the federal government, restore war-ravaged buildings, and raise money for additional building projects. The turn of the century welcomed numerous, relatively well-funded, and important expansions to the campus.

During this period of Storer's development, three libraries were instituted on the school's campus. The Roger Williams Library, located in Anthony Hall, served students, faculty, administration, and the general campus at large. By the 1890s, it was the primary holding site for over "four thousand five hundred volumes," with a substantial and varied complement of "papers, charts and magazines" available for use. In 1898, Baltimore's Enoch Pratt Library and Mary P. Smith of Nebraska collectively donated nearly 50,000 volumes to be added to the Roger Williams Library. After 1900, the central library incurred a period of expansion when its holdings surged

Lewis Anthony Industrial Building

to "over 500 volumes" and supplementary reading tables, work spaces, and current literature indices were added. In addition, each of the two key dorms had a library collection. In Myrtle Hall, the Dexter Library functioned as part of the reading room complex and contained three hundred volumes for use by female students. In Lincoln Hall, the boys' dormitory, the Wood Library boasted among its holdings a five-inch telescope, a "lunatelley," a 2.5-foot globe, several sets of charts, and a few pieces of chemistry equipment. Subscriptions to periodicals, reports, records, and journals that were supplied to campus libraries after 1900 were ever increasing. Between 1890 and 1920 when student activities were increased, members of "The Lincoln Debating Society," "Literary Society," and Woman's League," and declamatory and oratorical contestants required periodical subscriptions, since their activities revolved around current issues, trends, and topics of the day.

When Anthony Hall was damaged by fire in 1927, its library had to be relocated. Fittingly, it was moved to another building funded by the Anthony family, the Lewis W. Anthony Building, which had been built in 1903. The Board of Trustees intended that the Anthony building be used for its new Industrial Science Department programs. When the building was completed, it was a two-story limestone structure, dedicated two years later during a commencement program. When they donated money from their father's estate, three of the eight surviving Anthony children—Alfred Williams, Kate J., and another, unnamed in Storer's records—requested that the building bear their father's name.

When the time came to relocate the library from the old Anthony Hall, suggestions were made for updating the facility. These called for replacing of "1395 feet" of maple wood flooring, updating heating and lighting systems with accompanying fixtures, modernizing of bathroom accommodations, the purchasing of metal book stacks for library use, along with adding new furniture. The building also was in need of "a new concrete platform" and "a porch" to modernize and update the facility. By 1931, several of these suggestions had been honored by the

Anthony family. Modernized steam heating and water systems were installed, and the interior's hallways and rooms painted throughout, so that the Lewis W. Anthony building, previously used for manual coursework, was converted for library usage. It became the Lewis W. Anthony Library with the "name on the lintel," reflecting the Anthony family's financial support.

Another of the school's founding fathers likewise had his name attached to a building erected during the era. On September 29, 1889, the Harpers Ferry Free Will Baptist Church cornerstone was put in place to correspond with the Free Will Baptists' General Conference, although the church's construction was delayed for several years thereafter. It was not until M. B. Smith and J. Howard Gruby, executors, made an offer of $500 for the Silas Curtis estate that construction was resumed. According to the proviso accorded by Smith and Gruby, the church was to incorporate the Curtis surname. In 1892, the church was duly dedicated as the Curtis Memorial Free Will Baptist Chapel. Not unlike other buildings of the period, the church was made of brick set upon a limestone basement with a gray-black slate roof. The church also had a striking bell tower that was twelve feet square and fifty feet high. Southern pine and poplar were used to finish the church's interior. Perhaps more importantly, students enrolled in Storer's new Industrial Department were responsible for the construction. During its years of use, the church's dedicatory windows identified several individuals and youth societies that contributed to the church's creation, from inception to completion.

Growth and Change

Additionally, during the first decade of the twentieth century, the college had invested in, constructed, or managed several properties surrounding the campus in order to attract visitors and generate additional revenue for its coffers. An early 1920s property inventory indicates that these properties were used as residences for visiting boarders or teachers. Most of these structures were small dwellings comprising only one-and-a-half stories of living space. In 1906, for example, the "Shenandoah Cottage" was indemnified through the Phoenix Assurance Company for $700. The cottage was often used for private boarding, but in 1925 it was rented on a monthly basis for $50 to Ammon M. Rogers from Poolesville, Maryland. Another two-story bungalow was the Jackson Cottage, built in 1912. This small structure was chiefly used as a private residence for campus instructors. The Jackson Cottage was demolished three years after federal acquisition of the campus in 1960. The McDaniel, Robinson, Saunders, Sinclair, and McDowell cottages were likely used as needed for either additional income or residential space for teachers. The Sinclair and Saunders cottages were structurally different in that they possessed two stories instead of the traditional one-and-a-half story design.

Situated on "Lot 7" among campus properties was the White Cottage, owned by Lura Brackett Lightner. Although Lightner had verbally committed to deeding the property back to the Board of Trustees after she vacated it for use by incoming "white women

teachers," she did not fulfill this agreement. Instead, she eventually leased or rented the property to Mabel S. Brady and Elizabeth Brady Bird, both of whom were employed by the college at different times in many capacities. In 1909, plans were underway to construct a "one dwelling place" on the corners of Jackson and Fillmore streets, a parcel that was part of the original government acquisition in 1868. Dimensions for the wooden house are listed as thirty-two feet by thirty-two feet, with a comparable rectangular section shown as twelve feet by twenty-five feet projecting from the western façade. Designed as a two-story house with attic, the

Waterman House

Robinson Barn

house boasted ceilings that were ten feet high at its center. Funding for the house was given by the widow of Granville C. Waterman, who had been the principal at Pike Seminary in New York. Mrs. Waterman knew, therefore, the condition under which many of the denomination's administrators had lived. The Watermans' son, Reverend Dexter Waterman, taught "Scripture History and Butler's Theology" at Storer College for a period, and he was a member of its Board of Trustees, with his term expiring in 1890. The house was often referred to as either the "President's House" or the "Waterman House."

During the same period, the college had two barns on its property, including one near Anthony Hall, since the school was likely making use of livestock to teach courses in animal husbandry, biology, zoology, natural sciences, and botany. College catalogs for several consecutive years, beginning in 1903, demonstrate that such coursework was indeed available for students. Perhaps livestock were also required to demonstrate culinary preparations and slaughtering procedures for the school's collective consumption and public sale. A second barn, the Robinson Barn, located on the eastern side of Anthony Hall, was converted for use by students as a gymnasium.

As construction projects progressed, fires took their toll on two college structures. During April 1909, the original boys' dorm, Lincoln Hall, long used as a summer boarding facility, burned. The construction of the hall in 1870 had marked the first major physical undertaking by the Free Will Baptists to expand campus facilities and was the first joint venture between the Baptists, the bureau, and the boys who first enrolled in the school's programs. Its demise meant the end of an era. In 1910, a new dormitory was erected for boys attending the school,

New Lincoln Hall

known thereafter as "New Lincoln Hall." To this building project, Kate J. Anthony personally donated $1,000 and raised another $500.

When the fall term began in September 1909, the new building was structurally nearly complete, although heat, electricity, and bedding were not yet in place. Male students were "temporarily sleeping on the floor and eating in the girls' dormitory as the building neared completion. In a dedicatory service, the dormitory was renamed Brackett Hall to honor the school's first principal and superintendent of schools. When New Lincoln Hall was completed, the Free Will Baptists had constructed a three-and-a-half-story limestone building with nine windows along the building's frontage. This included a partial subterranean elevation to correspond with the hillside's rugged

DeWolf Industrial Building

topography. Eight years later, in 1918, the long-established tradition of the building as a boys' dormitory forever changed when it was reestablished as a dormitory for girls. The college experienced yet another fire when on October 24, 1927, the Anthony Memorial Hall burned.

Work on a new water supply line began in 1911. As reported by the *Storer Record*, a one-hundred-foot deep well, a pump room, and an updated pumping system manufactured by the Keewanee Company had been installed on campus. A six-thousand-gallon capacity water tank was placed in the basement of the Anthony Memorial Hall, with a corresponding cesspool on the eastern side of the hall. By 1915, a seventy-foot water tower with a fifty-thousand-gallon capacity replaced the former system. In 1920, masonry students erected the limestone "Soldiers'

Alumni Fence and Soldier's Memorial Gate

Gate" to honor alumni who had fought in World War I, while that same year carpentry students built an "Alumni Fence" to enclose campus grounds and walkways.

The masonry and carpentry students had been trained on campus in Storer's new "Industrial Department" after 1884. In 1891, the DeWolf Industrial Building was erected to serve as the home for vocational education. The building was named in honor of Alvah B. Dewolf, after his widow, Mary, donated $2,000 to complete the industrial project in 1887. By 1891, the Board of Trustees approved the construction of a east-west passageway from the back wall of the entrance hall in Anthony Memorial

John Brown's Fort had been purchased by a group of Chicago businessmen interested in reconstructing the fort for public exhibition at the Chicago World's Fair. At the expense of Miss Kate Field, a historically minded actress, journalist, and philanthropist, the structure was dismantled in Illinois and transported to West Virginia, where it was reassembled on the Alexander Murphy farm, outside Harpers Ferry. When Storer's Board of Trustees learned this news, a plan was spearheaded and set into motion by Reverend Alfred W. Anthony. The fort was purchased and relocated to the Storer College campus, where it was refurbished and reassembled east of Lincoln Hall for use as a museum the following year, in 1910.

Several improvements were

John Brown fort after relocation to Storer's campus next to New Lincoln Hall (later renamed in honor of Principal Brackett)

Hall to the DeWolf Industrial Building. The passageway was a one-story framed structure bound on the north by Anthony Memorial Hall and on the south side by the DeWolf Industrial Building.

Perhaps the most significant new addition to Storer's campus, however, actually had its deepest roots in the previous century. In 1909,

made to the structure. New flooring was laid, glass cases of museum quality were installed in which to exhibit local artifacts and war memorabilia, and an elevated gallery was added to increase the interior's physical space. For a considerable period, Storer's students were responsible for giving tours of the museum, an endeavor that afforded them not only a chance to learn and disseminate valuable historical information, but also an opportunity to practice elocutionary skills. In later years, the Storer College National Alumni Association erected a plaque on the building to officially acknowledge John Brown's raid, which had, in effect, led to educational opportunities for the American Negro, in addition to liberating both races from institutionalized slavery. To have John Brown's Fort resurrected on campus gave further proof that Storer College was dedicated not only to bettering the lot of its students, but also to ensuring that the history connected with the freedmen's social betterment would not be forgotten.

Nathan Wood Brackett Steps Down

Even as early as 1882–1884, Nathan Wood Brackett's appointments had doubled and, with a student body nearing three hundred, his responsibilities likely multiplied exponentially. Never did Brackett perform only one function at Storer. He was not only the school's principal and superintendent, but also the Board of Trustees' treasurer. This was in addition to many off-campus organizational affiliations and social obligations. By 1896, he had spent over thirty years as the principal of Storer, a span of time that had witnessed the emancipation of a people and their determined search for education, as well as the growth of their awareness that independence alone does not guarantee equality and rights. In the interim, freed blacks began to speak out against what they perceived to be miscarriages of justice or examples of continued

inequality. Ironically, one of the things some Storer alumni criticized was a decision made under Brackett's administration regarding the practice of summer boarders.

Practically since its inception, Storer had leased out rooms in its dormitories and in the other structures it owned to boarders, either year-round or during the summer, as a means of supplementing college income. By 1896, however, it had become obvious that the practice was no longer profitable. That year, the college's Board of Trustees voted to discontinue summer boarding at Lincoln Hall, which had provided lodging for African American visitors since the war because there was no other alternative available in the area. The practice, however, was maintained at other locations "for white visitors . . . even though these operations were also not profitable" complained former students. In August of that year, at an "Alumni and Friends" meeting, the decision was heavily criticized, with the most vocal of the attendees being John "J. R." Clifford, alumnus and editor of the Martinsburg newspaper, the *Pioneer Press*. According to one account, the editor "used the paper as a vehicle for his criticism of the discriminatory nature of the summer boarding operation and of Brackett's administration at Storer in general" with which Clifford most assuredly did not agree. Regardless of whether or not the summer boarding decision was discriminatory, did it reflect on Brackett's administration as a whole?

Although there is no definitive answer to that question, throughout 1897 Brackett contemplated retirement, and in 1898 he finally stepped down. Brackett did, however, push for an investigation by the Board of Trustees into Clifford's allegations, and in 1899, the ensuing report vindicated him. Yet the tide had turned. The alumni response and Clifford's pressing of the discriminatory issue "demonstrated that Storer's students and alumni were beginning to express their own views on the administration of the school," much like students at Fisk, Tuskegee, Spelman, and other institutions during the same period.

Henry McDonald

While the Board of Trustees began to search for Brackett's replacement, they selected an interim administrator. Faculty member Reverend Ernest Earle Osgood, identified in the Annual Catalogue of Storer College, 1897–98, as a teacher of "Biblical Literature, Physical Culture, and Oratory," was chosen for the position. After the Board of Trustees interviewed various candidates, in 1899 its members elected Henry Temple McDonald, an incoming member of the classics faculty as Brackett's permanent replacement. In addition to his administrative responsibilities, McDonald would teach "Biblical Literature, Physical Culture, and Oratory." McDonald administered Storer for the next forty-five years until 1944, with the advent of the school's first Negro administrator. A Free Will Baptist from birth, McDonald had been born in the Midwest but was actually a descendant of one of New England's old families and "remained proud of this New England heritage throughout his life." McDonald earned his bachelor's and master's degrees from Hillsdale College, where he made his first substantive connection to Storer College by courting, and later marrying, Elizabeth Mosher, the daughter of trustee Frances Stewart Mosher.

After graduation, McDonald began his career as a principal with a position at North Adams, Michigan (1897–99). Then in April 1899 he moved to the same job with Hillsdale City Schools. When he learned of the opening at Storer, McDonald applied for it, eager to continue a tradition begun with his family's long-established pro-abolitionist activism. McDonald believed it "fitting" that he would get the job at Storer, as he told his mother: "Father worked for the physical freedom of the colored people and I'm in a way carrying on the work he was engaged in by working for their intellectual freedom."

According to reports, however, when McDonald arrived in Harpers Ferry he was "not exactly pleased with the condition of the school."

He observed "serious problems" and suggested that "future prospects seemed somewhat bleak." Among the elements that McDonald apparently thought problematic were a small faculty (seven full-time and four part-time teachers), no courses beyond the high school level, lack of science labs and equipment, and a central library he deemed outdated. Moreover, despite the success of its Normal Department, enrollment as a whole was apparently on the decline. How could the college—so applauded, so cherished—be suffering financially? There is no single answer.

During the final years of Brackett's administration, the school's administration had announced concerns about the same issues noted as problems by McDonald. By 1895, the school's dormitories—which had routinely boarded upwards of two hundred students per year—were in desperate need of essential repairs. The water systems were in need of improvements to maintain a healthy framework of "water pipes, pumps, [and] cisterns" in proper working order campus-wide. Moreover, it was costing more and more money annually to insure campus buildings.

Aware that it was also growing increasingly expensive to heat the sprawling houses on campus, as well as the individual dorm rooms, Brackett had taken great care to remind students of the rising fuel costs during cold months. During the 1895 school term, costs for fuel had doubled campus-wide.

In the face of a stagnant curriculum and declining enrollment, the school apparently realized the need to hire more instructors to broaden curriculum offerings and therefore enhance the quality across the field of instruction for incoming students. The president believed that although the school was "painfully conscious" of the necessity "to keep pace with the times" by adding new courses of study or enlarging established departments, doing so would add to the institution's financial burden. Increasing the number of teachers was vital, but it also meant taxing an already overburdened budget.

The overriding concern was that "the credit of the institution must not suffer," yet financial duress was having a negative impact. In 1895, Brackett had announced in the *Storer Record* a general appeal for funding. The Free Will Baptists, however, were adamantly opposed to debt accumulation, so there was not much that Brackett alone could do to correct the school's financial situation. Thus, as the century drew to a close, the school struggled for financing.

How did this dire financial situation occur? To begin, one must consider the impact of the Free Will Baptists' opposition to debt accumulation, which made seeking outside or "loaned" monies virtually impossible. But two other factors contributed to declining financial support for Storer—growing doctrinal debates within the denomination and emancipation itself.

Changes within the Free Will Baptist denomination affected support for efforts like Storer. For the last years of Brackett's term, making the most effective use of donated monies was a constant theme, for the school remained largely dependent upon the donations garnered within the denominational community. The mail constantly brought contributions from denominational friends, families, alumni, and other supporters. Yet, on the whole, financial support from the Free Will Baptists declined, mostly as the result of doctrinal conflicts that led to dissension within the denomination, but also due to the loss of key leaders in New England. Historical records indicate that "by the late 1880's and early 1890's, [the denomination] itself was in the midst of a crisis that would ultimately result in its reunion with the mainstream Baptists in the early twentieth century" after several years in schismatic disunion.

Thus, no single factor created the financial problems experienced by Storer by the turn of the century; however, the job of correcting—or at least alleviating—them remained. McDonald, the first administrator called "president," immediately began improving the campus, expanding the faculty, improving the curriculum, and creating better conditions for the students across campus. In 1904, McDonald acknowledged that in "appreciation of the great work the school has done for the commonwealth," the West Virginia Legislature had helped finance additional and necessary curriculum changes by contributing a "small biennial appropriation" to the school's budget. Specifically, the 1903 Legislature had appropriated monies "in payment for industrial training," so that the college finally accumulated substantial funds with which to complete a building for industrial instruction. Although industrial training had taken place on campus in some form or another since the 1880s, the emphasis placed on its Industrial Department during the

1890s and beyond bound Storer to a growing trend in the American working world. The growing centralization of the department followed the addition of two other departments, one devoted to biblical instruction, the other to music.

RELIGIOUS EDUCATION AT STORER

The Biblical Literature Department was established by vote of the Board of Trustees during the board's May meeting in 1894. The department was endorsed by the Free Will Baptist Conference Board in 1895, with McDonald listed as the department's lead instructor. Storer's Biblical Literature Department added a dimension to the school's normal and academic curricula by providing qualifying students with additional religious training. Admission requirements to the department, which was primarily "intended to train candidates for the ministry or missionary work," were accordingly rigorous. Each applicant was "examined as to character, experience, and adaptation for the Christian work contemplated" by him or her. Any student caught using "tobacco in any form [was not] admitted to the department."

A two-year curriculum, the "Biblical Department" offered its "First Year" students a basic yet broad approach to Christian religious studies. "First Year" students had to learn the "Books of the Bible" and all the "Principal Characters and Events [of] Bible History." Students also were expected to learn about the "Apostolic Church" in conjunction with the "Life of Paul" along with the "Acts of the Apostles and the

Pauline Epistles. The major method of examination was "Essays" in order for examiners to fully explore students' collective skills and abilities to formulate effective rhetoric. Additionally, students were given "instruction in Bible and hymn reading," making further application of the school's curriculum offerings.

During the "Second Year" of coursework, students began to focus on the "Life of Christ in the four Gospels" with St. Luke. It seems that "First Year" students focused on the "Principal" elements of Christianity while the "Second Year" was reserved for a closer examination of the person of "Christ." The college's catalogues also indicated that "students were allowed to pursue a partial course in connection with their studies in college."

Some of Storer's graduates became religious leaders throughout the continental United States and abroad. In keeping with the doctrinal emphasis of the denomination, however, they did not all become Baptist ministers. Although it was administered by the Free Will Baptist denomination, neither the college nor its Biblical Literature Department attempted to indoctrinate its students in Baptist theology. This policy is consistent with the earliest standards established by Storer's mission teachers, who often attended a variety of churches. Guided by this established practice, students were therefore drawn to various denominations as graduates. They acquired appointments with Methodist Episcopal and African Methodist Episcopal churches, as well as with Regular and Free Baptist denominations, among others.

Other students, especially those preparing for foreign mission assignments, took the opportunity to pursue coursework in both the teacher education and religious programs. After graduation, several students were recruited by foreign missions to provide aid and render service to native Africans on their ancestral continent, a task that included establishing both churches and schools. In 1865, mission teachers in America were responsible for transforming classrooms, in which they taught reading and writing, into sanctuaries for religious "praying and learning." That did not change over time.

Students graduating from Storer's Biblical Literature Department were eager to impact the communities for which they assumed responsibility—and, by and large, they were successful in the task. The Rev. J. C. Newman, an 1880 graduate, reported that his congregation increased by sixty during the winter months. John Burrell accepted a church position in Shepherdstown, West Virginia, and in 1896 he identified "several candidates for baptism" at his church in that community. An 1893 graduate, John W. Hayes, left the area to enroll in the Divinity School at Howard University. Hayes was "granted a local license" to preach in his hometown of Pittsburgh while matriculating through the divinity program at Howard.

On February 3, 1895, in St. Joseph, Missouri, a young African Methodist Episcopal pastor and 1880 Storer graduate, Reverend Frank J. Peck, held a dedication service to commemorate the community's new church, which his congregation had long awaited, supported, and financed.

MUSICAL EDUCATION AT STORER

By 1905–6, Storer had added to its growing curriculum a Musical Department—a logical extension given its long-established tradition of musical and vocal training since the 1865 mission teachers discovered how beautifully their students could sing. In spring 1895, the Harpers Ferry Singers, a vocal ensemble formerly known as The Union Chorus, embarked on a fund-raising tour, much like Fisk University's Jubilee Singers. A strictly auditioned group of singers, Storer's touring vocal ensemble had been performing as a quartet since the 1870s and had become quite famous for their skill. So varied were vocal demands placed on the group that it became all the more imperative to follow a strict regime of auditions for singers who could perform *a cappella*. After its early success, the group was expanded to an octet. Two singers were assigned to each of four basic voice parts—soprano, alto,

tenor, and bass—although during more complicated arrangements (i.e., Renaissance motets and madrigals) the four basic voice parts were divided into eight independent voice lines. The octet likely was responsible for memorizing all of its performance music, since the three primary teaching methods for the period involved "recitation," "repetition," and "practice," tasks closely associated with exercises in both mental and physical discipline.

Don "The Little Giant" Redman, a jazz-roaring 1920 graduate

Since on its tours the ensemble offered to New Englanders what was perhaps their first direct contact with the Harpers Ferry school, students selected for the octet were presumably gifted.

An integrated instrumental ensemble poses on the north lawn of Storer.

Growth & Change

The tradition of strict training continued with the newly established Musical Department. Under the direction of Rev. J. R. Wood, free choral vocal lessons were required of all students, but those who were interested in pursuing additional training could enroll in fee-based private lessons. Students interested in instrumental lessons

Marion Virginia Johnson Reeler, 1947

could, under the tutelage of Miss Emma F. Johnston and for a quarterly fee of $6—with half payable at the beginning of the term, and half when the lessons were half over—become adept at the piano or the organ. As time and styles progressed, the variety of music lessons offered at the school grew. By 1914, for example, as guided by bandmaster John W. McKinney, Storer offered "instruction in band music, orchestra, and several glee clubs," an effort to accommodate student interest and proficiency. Storer graduated several accomplished and talented musicians. Before graduating in 1920, for example, Don Redman, a leading jazz composer and musician in the 1920s and 1930s, played in the Storer College band.

The addition of Biblical Literature and Musical departments was predictable in an institution such as Storer. Religious education and musical training both play important roles in preparing students to undertake missionary work or to teach school during this period. Another of Storer's curricular developments, however, was perhaps not only more unexpected but a bit more controversial. The rise of Storer's Industrial Department can be interpreted as the school's response to a growing national need, which was an administrative effort to ensure that the school's curriculum corresponded with society's industrial growth.

STORER'S ANSWER TO INDUSTRIALIZATION

From 1882 to 1892, Storer College received $630 from the State of West Virginia. It is likely that this sum indicates the state's intention to financially sponsor industrial-type training for Negroes at that period in time. The "self-dependence" promoted by the founders was given a new context by the perceived shortage of industrial workers at the end of the nineteenth century. The focus of the Industrial Age was changing the job market. Skilled labor, precision, accuracy, and efficiency were new areas of emphasis because of increasing mechanization and assembly-line production. Educational institutions realized the potential for institutional growth fueled by these new demands. How could Storer's students develop the skills necessary to meet changing workplace demands unless they had been offered "industrial" coursework?

In 1895, the *Storer Record* stated that industrial education was necessary because "the condition and wants of the people made it such in fact, at a very early day" so that the administration was inclined to include a curriculum for an Industrial Department out of necessity based on need.

The Woman's Commission was largely responsible for voting to paint several rooms in Brackett Hall, so that eventually the commission was responsible for painting almost forty rooms in compliance with campus wide improvement measures.

STORER'S ROLE IN INDUSTRIAL EDUCATION

In 1904, McDonald suggested that "as the needs of the times have changed and it has become apparent that normal work ought to be supplemented with other work, Storer has changed her Curriculum. From her founding the school has stood by the theory that honest labor never degrades a man. And so it has been very easy for the college to expand its work to include Industrial training." Since its earliest days Storer College's founders and fathers firmly believed that in order for young men and women to demonstrate balanced development, they must be directed not only toward moral growth alone but also intellectual and physical development.

Although Storer did not possess a formal Industrial Department when it first opened its doors, "the condition and wants of the people" made it such in fact, at a very early day. In its formative years, the school used these courses more as a way of teaching hard work, industry, and Christian morals. Given the state of the buildings and grounds during

the early years of the college, such training was a practical necessity. These earliest industrial students began ground-keeping tasks, repairing the buildings, and producing food on the farm. With this in mind, it is likely that Storer's industrial students were responsible for building cottages for residential and rental property on the grounds.

After students demonstrated their mastery of the cottage-type structure, they worked with larger, gradated building blueprints such as those for the Curtis Memorial Chapel. It is known that Old Lincoln Hall was one such early demonstration of student aptitude for building construction. When Lincoln Hall was first erected, for example, a large part of the building effort was done by a "young man connected with the school under the direction of a skillful ex-union soldier," possibly William Henry Bell. When Anthony Hall was being built in 1881, Hamilton Hatter was enrolled in the Academic Department, although he also served as the "chief assistant of the principal in the construction of the building." According to the spring 1895 edition of the *Storer Record*, the school's farm properties were managed in the same fashion.

In these early days, most female students attending Storer had developed some cooking experience prior to their arrival, but eventually they were exposed to other experiences as well. During the 1870–80 decade, Louise Wood Brackett perceived that several "young women had much less knowledge of the use of the needle, than of the art of cooking." As a result, Louise Brackett and some of the other teachers began to offer "instruction in sewing, mending, making button holes and in making over old garments," ensuring that female students and future teachers would transfer these skills to their own upcoming students.

When the Industrial Department was formally developed, one room was used exclusively to teach sewing techniques and accurate cutting methods. Women who learned quickly to "do plain sewing and buttonhole work well enough" were then advanced to the more difficult levels of cutting, since precise measurement and accuracy were required as students began working with whole-piece garments.

In 1886, the Board of Trustees approved an expansion of the Secondary Division to include coursework in domestic sciences, gardening, upholstery, printing, carpentry, and blacksmithing, all of which exposed students to practical applications of trade skills. Eventually, in 1893, "Domestic Sciences" became mandatory for female students, and five years later they were given an opportunity to enroll in a formal three-year "Domestic Science" program. In 1897, the Industrial Department was added as a separate formal division of the school.

When the Industrial Department was established, it included training in the domestic sciences, carpentry, blacksmithing, and other vocational subjects. The "Domestic Sciences" component fell under the direction of "a graduate of the School of Domestic Science in Boston," who offered "instruction in cooking and housekeeping to over seventy young women, and lessons in cooking to about twenty young men" enrolled in the program. The school's Carpentry Shop had "six benches with tools," while

students taking courses in the print trades worked in the Print Shop on a daily basis. After 1895, the institution included a blacksmith and shoe division, and it increased the capacity of the carpentry division by purchasing more advanced machinery and new tools. During each week, "five to six days" were invested in instructing and operating the department's carpenter shop and printing establishment. Students working in the latter shop printed the *Storer Record*, the school newspaper. After the college expanded its programs to include an industrial division, enrollment in that curriculum quickly increased to 137 students, fifty-five more students than in the Normal Department, which until then had consistently maintained the largest enrollment in the school's history.

STUDENT LOYALTY DURING CHANGE

Regardless of curricular changes at Storer College, foundational philosophies remained consistent. As the *Storer Record* notes in 1895, "perhaps the most marked characteristic of Storer College is its policy of developing self-dependence. Its aim is not to take up young men and women and educate them, but to make it possible for them to educate themselves. Hence among its many graduates there are no drones or dependents."

Another tradition, that of educating native Africans, began in the nineteenth century and was continued at Storer College for many years. During the school's last decade before it closed, several African students had arrived in Harpers Ferry to enroll at the school, largely due to recruitment by the administration, clergy, and graduates.

Those who graduated from Storer expressed a great fondness for their alma mater. In order to maintain an ongoing relationship with the school and former classmates, Storer graduates often submitted personal information to be published in the *Storer Record*. From its 1896 edition, for example, we learn that former student Bertie Reed Scott had lost "her daughter, Rosa, who died March 12th, aged eighteen years"; that Rebecca McArd (or McCord) Johnson 1873 visited with Mrs. Robinson at Storer's Camp Hill Cottage; and that Mary Franklin Clifford 1872 and Lucy Scott Brown were attended by Mrs. Franklin.

It is likely these and many other visiting students returned to Harpers Ferry for annual meetings. Some did not leave at all. Several former students were placed in charge of various aspects of college operation. Brown F. McDowell, for example, an 1879 graduate, was selected "to run the Morrell House the coming season" while also recalled to his home in Lexington, Virginia, to handle his mother's estate and final funeral arrangements after her death. By 1902, the alumni had formed a formal association, held annual meetings, and began to include alumni lists in the annual catalogue. In 1907, the Alumni Association organized a $500 Alumni Scholarship Fund.

Just as the alumni remained committed to the Harpers Ferry school, so did its former principal. In appreciation for their combined years of service to Storer College, the Board of Trustees granted Nathan and Louise Brackett permission to live for the duration of their lives in the house that bore their family name. In 1910, Nathan Brackett died there. In 1911, the Alumni Association "provided the inscription for a marble tablet" commemorating the contributions of their former principal, when Lincoln Hall was renamed Brackett Hall. For twenty-six years after her husband's death, Louise Brackett occupied an apartment on the second floor of the house. She died in 1936. Although Storer College had witnessed many alterations to the school since it had begun in a single, war-torn mansion, the death of Principal Brackett and his wife truly marked the end of an era.

"The aims and methods of [the college] have always been broad and catholic. To make religion a life rather than a profession, to magnify the importance of keeping the commandments, rather than cultivating the emotions, has been the steady aim of the management. On the executive committee there have been for years a Presbyterian clergyman, a Methodist and an Episcopal layman, all working in perfect harmony with the chairman and principal of the school. The institution has been honored by being selected at different times by an Episcopal bishop, and by a Presbyterian college president, as a place to fit for college African boys who were under their care."

*The **Storer Record**, 1895*

Growth & Change

THE MOVE TO COLLEGIATE STATUS AND THE GROWING CRISIS, 1921–55

The final phase of institutional development experienced by the school was marked by some of the same underlying issues that had been a part of its beginnings. Equality was a reality at Storer, but the world outside the college was still iniquitous. At Storer, in unprecedented numbers, students would proclaim their interests, needs, and desires by calling persistently for reforms and for a larger stake in the governance of the school they attended. The world was evolving, and the community that was Storer would have to do likewise. Among the changes that occurred were the election of the school's first African American president and the addition of more "colored" teachers, the creation of a women's commission, and the development of a collegiate division. There was also a raging debate about whether the college should be placed under the control of the state, and finally, there was the biggest transformation of all—the closing of Storer.

The Yale-educated Richard I. McKinney was Storer's first African American principal administrator; Henry McDonald is seated at the right of McKinney for the official class picture

CONSTANCY, CHANGE, AND THE CAMPUS

While the campus community as a whole had witnessed myriad changes during the previous thirty-some years of its existence, two elements remained virtually constant— the college's physical environment and its need for funding. On the positive side, by the third full decade of the twentieth century, although many of its aged buildings were in constant need of repair, the physical campus had developed admirably. With the acquisition of additional adjacent land and buildings, it had been given the opportunity to expand. On the negative side, Storer's need for financial assistance remained persistent, as notes from McDonald, the third president, clearly indicate.

THE CAMPUS, 1921–54

Anyone visiting Storer in the last three decades of its existence would have witnessed few alterations in the school's grounds or in its buildings, with a few notable exceptions, such as Cook Hall. Myrtle Hall became the men's dorm, renamed Mosher Hall in honor of Board of Trustees member and longtime supporter

A 1937 senior graduate pose

Frances Stewart Mosher. By 1941, the venerable Lockwood House had become an apartment building, used primarily by faculty members.

Among the older buildings, Anthony Memorial Hall took on an even greater role by serving as the home of new laboratories for the expanded science curriculum. In 1925, however, there was no flooring in the basement of the Hall, although space was made for a furnace room with "coal bunker" enclosure.

On October 24, 1927, Anthony Memorial Hall suffered serious damage from a fire, perhaps caused by the installation that same year of sophisticated steam heat and water systems. Schematics produced after 1927 illustrate piping along the side of the building, in addition to a fifty-thousand-gallon capacity water tower. The structural damage was substantial. Major floor and ceiling joists were fractured throughout the first- and second-story levels. Rafters and rooflines were essentially demolished. Weakened walls, floors, and basic framing were such that

the weight of the heavy steam radiators previously used to heat the building gave way, crashing through the floorboards from one story to the next. Estimates for repairs neared $60,000.

In January 1928, before these repairs could be completed, high winter winds caused the collapse of one end of the building. Exposed throughout the winter months to heavy snow, sleet, and the excessive winter winds atop Camp Hill, the Hall was in deplorable shape by the time workmen began to salvage the building. Seven months later, in August, repairs were frantically underway so that the structure could be ready for incoming students in September. Anthony Memorial Hall experienced two fires in 1937 and again in 1939. Students' classes and activities were continued in makeshift classrooms in recitation and sitting rooms, in addition to making use of what was, by then, available laboratory space.

Another important structure from the nineteenth century, New Lincoln Hall, was given a new lease on life in the twentieth. New Lincoln Hall was renamed Brackett Hall in honor of the school's first principal administrator after Brackett's death in 1910. Eventually, Brackett Hall was modernized for Storer's female students and when completed, could accommodate more than one-hundred women.

After 1936, however, Brackett House had been rented, at least in part, to generate additional revenue. The death of Louise Wood Brackett, who had been given an apartment on the second floor of the building in that same year, signified the closure of two aspects of

Growth & Change

Storer's history. The first was the presence of the first-generation Bracketts, and the second was the retirement of the first-generation Board of Instructors. In 1944, a section of the house was rented again, this time to victims of the town's October 1942 flood, for $25 per month. This was perhaps another demonstration of the "founders and fathers'" willingness to assist the displaced, who because of circumstances beyond their control were forced to depend on the charity of others.

Although the older buildings retained their symbolic value to the Storer community, the aging structures necessitated the sort of repairs that often drained the school's small budget. In 1938, new hardwood floors were installed in Brackett Hall, and the wiring was modernized at a cost of nearly $4,000. In 1939, rooms there were refurbished to update the "kitchen, teacher's sitting room, and superintendent's room." In 1942, after a small fire, electricians determined a 200 percent overload on the building's electrical system, and declared a need for future electrical maintenance and significant updating. In 1944, the slate roof on Brackett House began to leak. A metal roof was installed at a cost of $822.25, a princely expenditure that had to be approved by the school's treasurer, George B. Fraser. During summer 1944, even more repairs were made to the house, including additional wall plastering and much-needed electrical rewiring. In

The graduating class of 1934, dressed in formal black regalia, with underclassmen in contrasting color

October 1944, the McDonalds relocated from Anthony Hall into Brackett Hall. Mrs. McDonald was still living there at the time of the school's closure in 1955.

In 1927, President McDonald had requested that the Free Baptist Woman's Missionary Society assist the college with its next major construction project, erecting the Domestic Science Building. Society member Permelia Eastman Cook personally donated $15,000 toward

114

the project with the proviso that the society as a whole shoulder some of the financial burden and responsibility by matching this amount. The Free Baptist Woman's Missionary Society and the American Baptist Woman's Missionary contributed matching funds. The cornerstone for Cook Hall was laid, and the building, constructed of stone mined from the college's nearby limestone quarry, was erected beside the John Brown Fort Museum. The building was completed in 1940 and housed classrooms, dorm rooms, and an art collection. However, the domestic sciences did not prove to be much in demand at Storer, for by the second year of its existence the building was so underutilized that McDonald ordered it "partially closed" to conserve expenses. In an effort to make it more useful to the college community, the Board of Trustees decided to keep the building open as a dorm for majors in the Home Economics program and female seniors.

In 2003, Cook Hall Dormitory was still used as a dormitory for Park Service trainees by the National Park Service where "approximately 1500 trainees complete one- and two-week courses" as a part of the service's continuing educational program each year.

While the continued presence of historically important campus landmarks lent the school an air of establishment, one of the most unfortunate consistencies at

Storer was its persistent need for additional funding. This ultimately forced the Free Will denomination to rejoin the General Baptist Conference in 1911 after the denomination's self-imposed segregation from its conference in the nineteenth century over the issue of slaveholders in their midst. During the first decades after 1900, McDonald's administrative activities indicate that he was making routine plans for endowment funding in order to secure scholarships, laboratory equipment, and other facilities. At the end of World War I, the

Permelia Eastman Hall (formally Cook Hall)

General Baptist Convention initiated a five-year program (1919–24) designed "to raise a single budget to be divided among its various agencies through a General Board of Promotion and its Administrative Committee." This multiyear program, known as the "New World Movement," brought a shift in financial focus that worked to McDonald's advantage.

McDonald possessed a variety of fund-raising talents and a relatively keen business sense. He tried a number of approaches designed to bring more revenue to the school's coffers. Over the years, he maintained the policy of letting rooms and apartments in college buildings. In 1921, he sought to decrease fuel expenditures and increase available resources by suggesting the purchase of "a coal yard," an idea approved by Harry S. Myers, secretary to the General Board of Promotion of the Northern Baptist Convention. Myers noted with satisfaction that "it [the mine] apparently will pay for itself in two years." As it turned out, Storer was granted use of coal reserves owned by John Aglionby—the

THE GOLDEN TORNADO 1923-24
STORER COLLEGE, HARPERS FERRY, W. VA.

1923 Golden Tornadoes football team

Dittmeyer Coal Shed property that they then purchased for the sum of $100 in 1923.

McDonald's fund-raising efforts also included a marketing campaign designed to advertise Storer to the larger world. At some point after 1920, he developed a promotional brochure for the school entitled *Storer College Gives You Welcome*. The brochure provided students with the early historical background of Harpers Ferry, John Brown, and the college. In the brochure, McDonald emphasized that Storer College was established for "fostering education under positive religious influences" while "shaping the lives of several thousand men and women" in order to "give a better vision of the meaning and possibilities of larger living." He also maintained that the college was not only "sending leaders to Africa, [but also] South America and widely over the United States." From the school's inception, it "has been active in cultivating better inter-racial relationships and its sons and daughters have made their mark in all the useful walks of life," McDonald concluded his promotional brochure with an invitation to potential students and "friends." "We bid you linger and feel the inspiration of our rimming mountains and catch the refrain of the lovely Shenandoah, 'Daughter of the Stars.'"

McDonald also cultivated close ties with individuals and philanthropic associations that had long supported the college's finances. His April 1, 1925, letter to Dr. James H. Dillard, a representative of the Slater Fund, stands today as an excellent example of a fundraising letter, a request that is as cordial as it is persuasive. "I have read with deep interest the annual report of the work done the past year by the Slater Fund," McDonald begins his missive. "It is certainly a very fine expression of wisely directed philanthropy." After noting that the Slater Fund was not currently supporting schools in West Virginia, McDonald subtly broaches the topic: "I am wondering whether or not as a result of your knowledge of the work and needs of Storer College, we would not come within the number of worthy schools, which might be included in the scope of those being assisted." Subtly again, the request is made: "I need not mention the great increase in the cost of maintaining such an institution and the changing attitude of those interested in such work as is being done in these schools. You well know of all that. Our need for help is not unique: it is perennial. Accordingly I am writing to ask that Storer be numbered among the schools to be assisted the coming year."

Despite his apparently continuous dedication to the task of seeking additional funding, McDonald faced an uphill battle that would extend into the next decade. In the "General Information" section of the 1937–38 catalogue, for example, at the end of a list of landmark dates, was an ardent plea. "There are definite and pressing needs. The order of their importance is immaterial, because all are so vital. They are: A fire proof library building and books; a science hall, domestic arts building, greatly increased working and permanent funds." And in a headnote to its "Scholarships and Prizes" section, the catalogue notes that "Storer College can be of much greater service to poor, but worthy, young men and women, if it were enabled by additional scholarships to offer larger opportunities here. We earnestly urge the founding of additional scholarships" to aid students with potential yet with limited means. By the 1940s, such pleas had disappeared from the school's catalogue, but the fact that they existed in earlier versions indicates the degree to which, well into the twentieth century, after seven decades of existence, Storer College still struggled financially. There would be many more challenges to face before the college closed its doors in 1955.

COLLEGIATE STATUS, PRE-MEDIC COURSEWORK, AND THE WOMAN'S COMMISSION

The addition of a formal Industrial Department to supplement the "hands-on" training courses that had always existed in some form at the school meant that Storer was responding to a marked educational trend for African Americans, and one that had its detractors. Some expressed concern that by teaching students industrial rather than "higher" skills, the model perpetuated their subservience to a class of (generally) white individuals who were possessed of a classical education and thus truly fit for the professional careers denied their black brethren.

Almost diametrically opposed in philosophy, intent, and tenor to this curricular change toward Industrial Education are two developments that occurred at the school in the twentieth century. The first was the school's assumption of junior college status in 1921, and the second was an emphasis on scientific study that included a "pre-medic" curriculum. The changes are indicative of efforts by the Storer administration to better define the school's mission. Storer was trying to find a place for itself by serving as preparatory training for dental, medical, pharmaceutical, or other professions, in addition to chemical and organic research-based careers included under the broad umbrella of science.

JUNIOR COLLEGE STATUS

Obviously, the pre-medic course was not part of a secondary school program, but rather a key element in the school's relatively new collegiate division, which had begun in 1921 with the establishment of a junior college curriculum. Spurred by the "original vision of Storer's founders," McDonald had begun as early as 1918—most probably to

assist returning soldiers—an effort to establish for Storer junior college status. After a period of inaction by the Board of Trustees, for the 1921–22 school year, the college admitted six freshmen, three of each gender, into its junior college division, although the school's new status would not be official until 1922. This approval came after the Board made clear that for the present coursework would be confined to the junior level. The program included standard courses in English, Math, Chemistry, History, Sociology, Psychology, and Ethics, to mention a few. Storer's junior college status was based on requirements and regulations according to the state's Free School System and Board of Education. The college's curriculum and programs were "recognized as standard by the State of West Virginia," and so students were graduating from a recognized program. In 1923, Watson David Hill became the first student to graduate from Storer's junior college program, although he did not in fact possess an associate-level degree.

Associates of Arts titles were not granted to students until 1937, after McDonald had managed to convince the Board of Trustees that making such "rewards" possible would assist students "in applying to other colleges and . . . [increase] the prestige of the program" at the same time. Still, according to the Board's mandate, the college could make no reference to the official granting of a "degree"—merely a "title."

That would change, however, during the 1939–40 academic year, when Storer began what it called a "full college" course of study. Although it was still possible for a student to acquire from the college a two-year degree, the four-year program began to offer degrees in Language and Literature, Natural Sciences, Social Sciences, Education, and Pre-Medic subjects. Students intent on pursuing the Elementary Collegiate or Standard Normal certificates also could still do so.

THE PRE-MEDIC CURRICULUM

As McDonald notes in a 1925 letter to Kate Anthony requesting funds to create labs to train students for the medical profession. Writes McDonald: "Students here are asking for courses in science which will meet the Pre-Medical requirements of the American Medical Association. By being enabled to take such work here, where expenses are minimum, some will be enabled to take medical, dental and pharmaceutical course, who otherwise would never do so. There is the greatest need for such professional men. Among white people already there is a shortage of medical men; much more is it the fact with the colored people."

By 1936, the "Pre-Medic" program was fully established. The school's catalogue was accompanied by a note suggesting that it had the full blessing of the State of West Virginia: "The State of West Virginia is anxious that students of its colleges be thoroughly prepared for entrance upon medical courses. Most colleges are requiring three years of college work for such preparations. To meet this demand Storer College is offering a full pre-medic course" for students interested in this field. The program involved a specific academic plan that focused on work in biology, zoology, organic chemistry, embryology, histology, and mammalian anatomy, among other courses.

The "Pre-Medic Course" was designed to involve students in three years of coursework with professors Briscoe and Johnson. Briscoe taught the categorical biology courses while Johnson taught the chemistry courses. During the "Freshman Year," students had to take eight hours of "General Inorganic Chemistry," and four-hours each of "General Biology and General Zoology." The freshman also had to take six hours each of "Mathematics" and "English." The first year of study involved a total of twenty-

"We have not been able to have a manual training teacher since the War, because of the large salary demanded by such teachers. Only at irregular times have we been able to have a domestic science teacher. We are doing Junior College work. The demand for that is increasing. There is a vital need for the doing of such work here, and we are doing it to the best of our ability. But we much need additional laboratory room and equipment. For the fitting up of needed laboratories we need now about $5000. This year by most rigid economy we have been able to gather and spend between $800 and $1000 for new equipment."

From a letter from Henry Temple McDonald to Dr. James H. Dillard, April 1, 1925

eight hours of coursework. As expected, advancing coursework stipulated that students remaining for the sophomore year had to take three hours of "Qualitative Analysis" and three hours of "Quantitative Analysis," with another eight hours of coursework set aside for

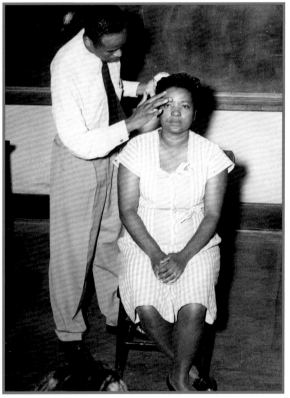

Models volunteered to demonstrate anatomical points of instruction

"Vertebrate Zoology" and "Mammalian Anatomy." The sophomore year involved twenty-one total hours to complete. It was during the sophomore year that students also studied "Mechanics, Heat and Sound," and "Light, Electricity, and Magnetism." Students enrolling for the junior year in the "Pre-Medical Department" took three elevated sciences—"Organic Chemistry," "Histology," and "Embryology."

Storer's 1937 catalogue stated on its title page that the school was "A Junior College For Colored Youth: With Pre-Medical . . . Departments." The title page was even redesigned to give particular emphasis to the "Pre-Medical Department." Students enrolled in the "Pre-Medical Department" incurred additional laboratory expenses. The "Laboratory Fee" range was between $3 and $6. For the analysis category classes students paid $3. "Physics" lab work was provided for students at a cost of $4 "Qualitative and Quantitative Analysis" lab fees were $3 each while the "Biology and Organic Chemistry" laboratory fees were the most expensive listed, at $6.

Senior College Status

When the State of West Virginia conferred upon Storer College all the rights and privileges of a state-accredited institution in 1934, the college began to experience the "permanent blessings" of John Storer's vision because it was fulfilling his original "deeply absorbing plan" to establish a college in the South "to benefit the colored race." The school offered students opportunities to enroll as candidates in degree programs in "Bachelor of Arts and Sciences," "Bachelor of Science in Home Economics," "Associate of Arts in Music," and "Bachelor of Arts in Education," with an increasingly difficult curriculum to coordinate with the degrees.

Students enrolled in the "Bachelor of Arts and Sciences" degree took several consecutive hours of biology, English, mathematics, psychology, social science, ethics, history, and foreign language. The "Bachelor of Science in Home Economics" degree also incorporated biology, English, history, physical education, psychology, and economics.

However, during the third and fourth years, students turned toward their concentration and took bacteriology, organic, and physiological chemistry. They also then incorporated child care and training, family, and public speaking, with electives in textiles, art, foods, materials and methods, home management, directed teaching, educational psychology, dietetics, and the history of education.

An "Associate of Arts in Music" included sight singing and notation, ear training, and oral dictation, along with harmony. Music students also took methods, psychology, aesthetics, English, and foreign languages in order to complete the program. For the "Bachelor of Arts in Education" degree, students took a total of 128 hours to fulfill requirements and graduate. The course requirements, at this juncture, were quite substantial in range. These included general coursework such as English, literature, history, and economics to the more degree-specific philosophy, sociology, tests and measurement, problems of child adjustment, principles and management. Students also took ninety hours of mandatory observation and directed teaching in the school's "Nursery" school. Students enrolled in the "Bachelor of Arts in Education" program fulfilled their "Observation and Directed Teaching in the Elementary Subjects" course at the Grand View School located in Bolivar, West Virginia. The college catalogue stated that "although the work of the Junior and Senior years is elective, students must pursue such courses as will complete the requirements in their major and minor fields" of study in order to meet the degree require-

ments for these programs of study. Therefore, the teaching candidates particularly had to fulfill the specified number of hours required for practice teaching in the college's elementary-level laboratory school.

THE WOMAN'S COMMISSION

While curricular changes might have taken center stage during this period, another change— this one more sociopolitical in nature—also

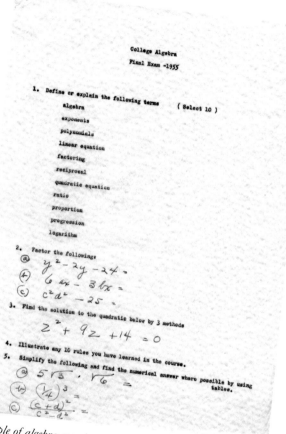

Example of algebra examination

occurred with the creation in 1938 of a Woman's Commission for female students and faculty members. Immediately upon its inception, the Storer College Woman's Commission began to address the needs of young women on campus and, over a period of years, made several general improvements to the girls' dormitory. In addition, the school turned to the Woman's Commission when renovations, repairs, or redesigning of college buildings became pressing. It was largely responsible for voting to paint several rooms in Brackett Hall, so that eventually the commission was responsible for painting almost forty rooms in compliance with campus-wide improvement measures.

The commission continued to exert a powerful presence on campus. For example, in 1945, the Woman's Commission was put in charge of renovating the uppermost story of Brackett Hall to make the rooms habitable for the school's growing female population. In 1945, the "Minutes of the Woman's Commission" identified that the commission approved to accept the responsibility for improving the flooring on the third floor, and locating work-men to do the work of sanding, refinishing, and varnishing.

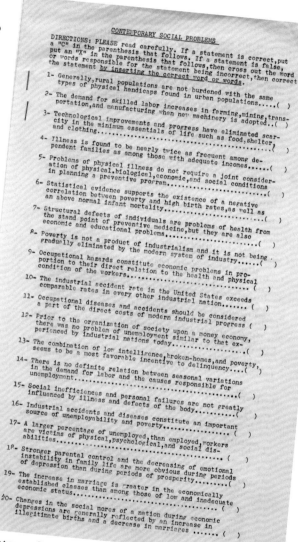

Contemporary Social Problems Examination

Transitions and Endings

THE "TAKEOVER" DEBATE

Storer's educational emphasis shifted from the preparatory and secondary work that preoccupied its efforts during the first six decades of its existence. As early as 1919, McDonald reported his belief that the school's goal "should be to serve as a good regional high school for black students who wanted to go on to college." The Preparatory Department, therefore, was eventually developed. Later two- and four-year degrees, in addition to extension work in such areas as vocational agriculture, became the new focus of the school on Camp Hill. The Board of Trustees was passive in its own efforts to enact key changes at the school, and so without McDonald's vision and active pursuit of these curricular changes, it is unlikely that Storer College would have established itself as a "college" in the modern sense of the term. Nonetheless, McDonald's tenure at Storer was not without its controversies, the most pronounced of which involved the efforts of some Board of Trustees members to place the school under the control of the State of West Virginia.

Although the school's new junior college status was exciting, it did not at first attract a large number of students. Enrollment in the program remained low in the 1920s. Although the school still received support from long-time "friends," including individuals and philanthropic organizations, and funds from Baptist organizations and the state, it

Winter scene on Storer's campus with view from north to south

continued to struggle financially as its curriculum expanded. One historical account indicates that although by 1926, the state legislature's annual contribution had increased to a bit over $6,000, this sum "did not even cover half the salaries of the faculty and administration." The Free Will Baptist-Home Mission Society contributed only about $2,500 annually. Additional monies from the Woman's Baptist Home Mission Society were greater—$3,000—but used only for programs that served female students. The situation had become so dire that at the end of fiscal year 1925, Storer College's combined contributions from these three main sources totaled $12,096.58, while its operating expenses totaled $61,387.62—an astounding deficit of $49,291.04. Boarding fees, tuition, and income from the school's farming enterprises, property investments, and donations made up the remainder. One thing remained constant— tuition would not be raised sufficiently to cover expenses. In fact, Storer's mission was built expressly upon the foundation that it should "keep tuition and expenses low so even poor students could attend" and not be "debarred from the privileges of study" for lack of funding. This had been the school's historic position since its formal organization.

This first hesitant decade of junior college coursework was marked by a conflict between McDonald and select Board of Trustees members, particularly Dr. Alfred Williams Anthony—son of the school's long-time benefactor Lewis W. Anthony—over the school's administration. According to reports, Anthony deemed McDonald's presidency "inefficient," and the extended conflict eventually focused on the question of whether the State of West Virginia should assume control of the college.

At the May 1919 Board of Trustees meeting, Anthony made his opinions clear to other Board members. The matter seemed to die for a time because no action was taken, and Anthony apparently tried to smooth things over with McDonald. He wrote the president a letter in which he expressed the fear that his motives had been "misinterpreted," and "argued that he only meant to point out where work still needed to be done to keep Storer headed in the right direction." McDonald, school treasurer Lura (Brackett) Lightner, and Rhode Island trustee Alice M. Metcalf, however, were among those who believed that Anthony's remarks were critical of the administration. In a letter to Anthony, Lightner notes the logic of his comments, but also commends McDonald's efforts. Lightner had inherited the treasurer's office from her brother, Nathan, when he died in 1910. This perhaps gave added weight and value to Lightner's opinions and criticisms.

Battle lines were drawn, complicated by the fact that Anthony's assessment of the situation did

One of Storer's "celebrity" students poses against the backdrop of eighty-eight keys

Operatic production and performance was common as shown here. The cast pose for an official picture before the staged performance of Handel's Saul.

school's 1868 charter, which had contributed three elements to the present problem. It divided administration between a Board of Trustees and a five-member Executive Committee, including members of the board who lived nearby who monitored daily operations; it made the president of the school a member of both groups; and it invested the president with "extensive decision-making powers." The Executive Committee met monthly, while the larger group met annually—but rarely with all members present. Because the former group was responsible for day-to-day operations and since some trustees failed to attend the regular annual meetings, many of them were not aware of the Executive Committee's actions. In addition, the Board of Trustees seldom took decisive actions. As a result, by the 1920s, the Executive Committee had gained strength, and McDonald "was making many of the daily decisions . . . essentially on his own" without much input from other members. The naming of local individuals to the Executive Committee further strengthened McDonald's administrative position and by 1921, he "was practically assured that his wishes would be followed in the day-to-day administration of the school."

not encompass the full realm of problems confronting Storer. Whereas his comments suggested the problems were administrative, McDonald, Lightner, and others who worked more with the day-to-day operations of the school could have pointed out additional issues that compromised Storer's success, including an aging physical plant, inconsistent funding for expansion and programs, and administrators and faculty being stretched too thinly. Regardless, by the May 1920 Trustees meeting, Anthony expressed feeling "isolated" from other board members and began "to look for allies" among other trustees.

The reality of the situation indicates that both factions had some reasonable issues. The Anthony-McDonald conflict was actually rooted—although neither would have recognized it, perhaps—in the

Transitions and Endings

The last straw for Anthony came in 1921, when he learned that without consulting the board, McDonald had undertaken to raise funds for a new gym. After announcing the news to students, faculty, and alumni, McDonald—perhaps sensing "he had overstepped his bounds"—asked for and received the board's blessing at their May meeting, at which Anthony was not in attendance.

By 1925, tensions regarding the school's administration and precarious financial situation were high. Anthony and two other trustees affiliated with the Free Will Baptist denomination—George Hovey and Charles White—hit upon a plan they believed would keep the school afloat so it could continue to fulfill its mission. They would turn control of it over to the State of West Virginia.

In 1926, McDonald joined other presidents of Baptist schools for "colored youth" at an Atlanta conference designed to consider the widespread funding shortfalls. Records indicate that "it was agreed that the best approach would be a united five-year fund-raising drive with a goal of five to six million dollars." Storer's share of the sum would amount to roughly $400,000, with $150,000 of that amount devoted to building initiatives. Unfortunately, that plan was quashed by the American Baptist Home Mission Society, whose leaders expressed the belief that the organization was already overextended.

In 1927, Anthony and the "takeover" faction of the board began querying state officials about the idea. Some of McDonald's supporters—including alumna Coralie Franklin Cook, then on the faculty of

Howard University—began to marshal their forces, an effort that involved recruiting students and raising funds.

Yet, the matter was still to come to a head. When it did, ironically, it involved the very building that bore the Anthony family name. After fire destroyed much of Anthony Memorial Hall in fall 1927, the board disagreed over whether it should be repaired, Anthony agreed that until they could decide on the hall's future usage, no money should be expended on it. At Anthony's insistence, the building "was left to the elements" during the harshest months of the year. It took a special meeting of the Board of Trustees in February 1928 for McDonald to prevail. Anthony Memorial Hall would be rebuilt—and the issue of state takeover, also discussed, was tabled temporarily.

At the regular May meeting that year, though, the plan was the central focus and a committee was formed to study the idea. When the trustees next met at a special meeting in November of

During the first decades of the twentieth century, Storer graduates began to strike more creative poses for graduation.

that year, two reports were submitted, one supporting the plan, the other opposing it. Among the resolutions proposed by the latter report was a plan to "keep the school's present Baptist affiliation with such state aid as could be had," an idea voted down by five to two, with two members (McDonald and J. C. Newcomer, Celeste Brackett's husband) abstaining. By the same margin, a second resolution—to place the college under state control—was then passed and a committee was formed, on which McDonald agreed to serve, to undertake the transfer. The fate of Storer College seemed determined.

A bill regarding the transfer of the college made it to the second reading in the House of Delegates in February 1929. At about the same time, McDonald appeared before the Finance Committee on an allegedly unrelated matter. Soon after, a decision was announced that the bill would not be passed that year. Although McDonald's original presentation of the bill to the legislature the previous fall reportedly had been fair-handed, in the end—once passage became a real possibility—did he argue it down? Such an allegation was made and McDonald denied it, but the fact remains that the potential transfer of Storer would be postponed for at least two more years.

In the end, Anthony discussed with Baptist officials the possibility of removing McDonald, but then resigned from the board himself as a result of what he called "challenges and attitudes towards me as President of the Board for holding and maintaining these opinions." Thomas E. Robertson (Mary Brackett's husband) replaced him as president and then, learning that Anthony planned to use him politically, supported McDonald. Ultimately McDonald remained president of Storer College.

THE GREAT DEPRESSION

Most of those who attended Storer College did not come from wealthy families, as is indicated by the school's endeavors to supplement its students' tuition monies and provide them with part-time jobs. In fact, records show that most of Storer's students came from poor families. By 1932–33, West Virginia had cut the college's annual appropriation by a little over a third, reducing it from $17,500 to $12,000, which meant that much tuition aid was lost.

It was difficult to keep students in school when they could not afford to be there. Nonetheless, the school did try to assist its students financially. The president noted: "We secured some financial assistance from alumni and friends, we made liberal scholarship grants, whenever possible and we created jobs, wherever there was the slightest excuse" to help students in need. McDonald summed up the state of the country in general and the trials faced by the least empowered segments of society, blacks in particular: "An impoverished people cannot send their sons and daughters to college."

Storer's enrollment dipped, waned, and showed little promise of rebounding throughout the 1930s, hitting a low during 1938–39, when McDonald reported "the number of students withdrawing for financial reasons had been especially high." That year's enrollment dropped to 122. In an effort to combat the problem, the school financially assisted 102 students to the total of $7,822.74. It seems clear that many who might have wanted to pursue a degree were unable to do so. Storer's long-standing financial difficulties compounded the problem. Armed with good intentions and a true desire to help as many students as possible, how could it accomplish this worthy goal with so little money?

HENRY MCDONALD'S PATERNALISM

On more than one occasion, Henry McDonald revealed the traditional paternalistic perspective that characterized most of his peers. In a 1925 letter to Alfred W. Anthony, the son of Lewis Anthony, McDonald recounts the resignation of one of Storer's teachers, Harriet Church. He suggests that "wear and tear" seemed to correspond with teaching in a school for colored students. "Colored people with rapidly

Henry Temple McDonald

increasing feelings of self sufficiency and all too manifest self assertion, are not moved by the fine feelings of appreciation which were everywhere, when I came here," McDonald said. He then moved to what appears to be a suggested solution to the "wear and tear" placed on "white teachers," and one he clearly opposes—increasing the number of black teachers. "I want to stress, that white trustees may be conscious of the situation, the idea of not allowing the relative number of colored teachers here to be increased," he writes. "We must have good teachers, and we must pay salaries which will make it possible for white people to teach here." In letters dated as late as 1943, McDonald still held strong to the paternalistic view of education and argues that "whites should still play a leading role" in the education of blacks. Without question, his views derive from a sense of racial superiority. As he noted, "I still think our ancestry, training and larger fitness enable us—white people—to do something for colored students, which they can get no other way."

Throughout the 1940s, the Board of Trustees had become more aware of the great power McDonald wielded at Storer, and its members gradually moved to shift such power. In 1941, the board created a dean of instruction which divested McDonald of his role as dean of men and Elizabeth McDonald of hers as dean of women. In 1942, McDonald resigned as the school's treasurer. Later, he left both the Finance and Executive Committees. By 1943–44, the president "had been relieved of most of his duties," and at the end of that term, he resigned.

RICHARD ISHMAEL MCKINNEY, AN IVY LEAGUE, NEGRO PRESIDENT

Richard Ishmael McKinney

Once more, the Board of Trustees was confronted with locating a suitable administrator to assume the president's duties and responsibilities. In 1944, the Board of Trustees selected Richard Ishmael McKinney as McDonald's successor. He was well qualified. He possessed a Bachelor's degree from Morehouse College, a B.D. from Andover Newton Theological School, and a Ph.D. from Yale University. From 1934 to 1935, he served as a Baptist minister, then he accepted a teaching position at Virginia Union University, where in 1942 he became dean of the School of Religion. For Storer, McKinney was not only the first Negro president in the history of the school but also the first to hold a doctoral degree (Ph.D.) to be considered for the executive position by the Storer College Board of Trustees.

Despite being highly qualified, McKinney's welcome at Harpers Ferry was less than congenial. During a 1999 interview, the former college president recalled his first night in Harpers Ferry, when a burning cross welcomed him on his front lawn. Before he accepted the administrative appointment, McKinney knew full well he would be fighting the tide of local sentiment, yet he "began his administration full of optimism and ambitiously set to work to bring [the school] up to the standards of the modern four-year college" when he arrived on campus.

Under McKinney, the school reenvisioned itself as a "training ground for young African American men and women who would be leaders in the continuing struggle to achieve equality in society." Together, McKinney and the faculty devised a new mission statement. It stressed "a liberal education in a Christian environment" and impressed upon students that they must be "responsive to the challenge of leadership in the reconstruction of society along lines of the best in the democratic tradition."

The school's 1949 bulletin articulated the joint vision of McKinney and faculty in a series of ten objectives, which stated Storer's goal to address the whole student: intellectually, physically, spiritually, and socially. As a result, McKinney worked to give students more of a voice at the school. He established a local chapter of the NAACP and helped form a Student Government Association, which guaranteed that students would work cooperatively with faculty to shape the direction of Storer.

Transitions and Endings

McKinney also pushed forward with the goal of making Storer a noteworthy four-year institution. In 1947, in response to the fact that "more and more students were asking for pre-medical courses," a Science Building was constructed offering additional laboratory facilities for scientific experimentation. He also worked diligently on gaining regional accreditation in an effort to shape the transition for Storer into a four-year modern college. In 1946, West Virginia accredited Storer's B.A. in Elementary Education, as well as the English, home economics, science and social science sections of its secondary education division.

During McKinney's administration, two other important changes occurred. First, the number of African American teachers on the faculty increased. Secondly, via a developing relationship between McKinney and one of the school's most famous graduates, Nigerian President Nnamdi Azikiwe, Storer strengthened its ties between the United States and the African continent.

The addition of African American faculty in retrospect seems a logical change but one that was very long in coming. Of the eighteen active faculty members under McKinney, "at least 11 . . . were African American," including the president. With the increased hiring of "colored teachers," Storer truly became an integrated faculty. This trend did not arrive without an accompanying sense of unease. It had always been the intention of the Baptists to "gradually" withdraw from the "Southern enterprise" when "colored students were fitted to become teachers and preachers." Then "they would take the places of northern workers, and the schools and the churches [would be] supported by the people residing there." However, as the number of black faculty members increased, some white teachers had a problem coping with this evolution.

Nnamdi Azikiwe, the student

It is likely that tensions were also provoked by the second change that occurred under McKinney, which carried with it far more wide-reaching political and racial implications. Strengthening ties with Africa implied a certain level of activism that probably made some elements of the Storer community uncomfortable. The connection between Storer and the African continent was not new, however, but had been made much earlier. Under McDonald, students had been recruited from Africa. Several African missions under the direction of various denominations had sent Africans to Storer for their education. McDonald had strengthened and cultivated positive relationships with missionaries working in African regions.

Additionally, advanced sciences professor, Madison Spenser Briscoe, who taught at both Storer College and Howard University, had, through his laboratory investigations during the 1930s and 1940s, "bridged the North American and African continents in an effort to advance public health standards." This was during a time when public health medicine was not fully recognized as a separate branch of medical science by the medical community at large. Both McDonald and Briscoe knew Azikiwe, but under McKinney's administration the relationship between the African native and the school in Harpers Ferry took on an entirely new dimension. Azikiwe had been a student there for two years (1925–27) before financial difficulties forced him to withdraw and enter Howard University in Washington,

Nnamdi "Zik" Azikiwe in his formal attire as the High Owelle of Onitsha

D.C. (1927–29), where more lucrative job opportunities existed for students working their way through school. By 1929, Azikiwe entered Lincoln University, graduating a year later with a bachelor's degree in political science. While at Lincoln, he made the acquaintance of Thurgood Marshall and Langston Hughes. Marshall became the first African American Supreme Court justice; the latter, Hughes, was an esteemed, sociopolitical leader in the Harlem Renaissance through his numerous consciousness-raising essays and inspirational poetry.

Azikiwe's choice of political science as a major indicates not merely a casual interest but rather a life choice. That choice would be molded further by subsequent studies in journalism at Columbia University, an M.A. in religion and philosophy from Lincoln in 1932, a master's degrees in anthropology and political science at the University of Pennsylvania (1933), and a Ph.D. at Columbia. In the mid-1930s, with multiple degrees to his name and a strengthening dedication to social and political issues, Azikiwe returned to his native Africa. Immediately, he became involved in politics, forming a political party dedicated to liberating Nigeria from British colonial rule. In 1960, Azikiwe would finally see Nigeria become independent and himself become its first indigenous governor-general and commander-in chief.

Azikiwe was devoted to Storer from his early professional career. Consequently, in 1947, he was invited to address Storer students as a commencement speaker and presented a speech that was a rallying cry to activism through social leadership. Dr. Azikiwe challenged students to live meaningful lives through strict democratic practice. His objective was to prompt students to become more actively engaged—not only with their democratic society but also to develop within themselves an understanding and connection with the democratic process. After Azikiwe delivered the commencement speech, Storer College conferred upon him "one of only two honorary degrees" bestowed by the institution.

In spite of many obviously successful initiatives, McKinney faced rising criticism from members of the Board of Trustees despite the progress he had made in improving faculty and student relations at Storer and in making the student body more cognizant of their civil and political responsibilities. Although the school had never been financially stable, under McKinney the deficit that had begun during the last years of McDonald's tenure grew more pressing. Moreover, McKinney had been unable to get full accreditation for the school because the criteria for colleges and universities accredited by the South Central regional accrediting body were beyond the scope of Storer's means. The mandatory endowment alone, over $100,000, for such colleges excluded Storer's membership. By 1948, Storer's financial difficulties had created a wedge between its predominantly white executive Board of Directors and its first Negro president and direct administrator. Many board members who had parted ways with McDonald under less than cordial circumstances now began to contact him for opinions, insight and information-gathering. Additionally, it must be pointed out that the board held a white majority and that McDonald, who remained

embittered about his resignation, possibly expressed negative comments about the school's new president.

The tensions between McKinney and the school's board would ultimately reach a crisis. With a chronic financial deficit and a board that maintained paternalistic tendencies, McKinney felt that his position was growing tenuous. He was caught between the board's politics and the school's advancement. McKinney was a true academician, and the progress of his school and his students was his primary objective.

When the Board of Trustees met in 1949 McKinney offered his resignation, and although the members refused to accept it, they also initially failed to reelect him. Judge Thomas Robertson, chair of the Finance Committee, made a motion that proposed the board not reelect McKinney. Although the board subsequently voted to reinstate McKinney, it became clear that he had at least one vocal enemy among its members—and that consequently his days as president were numbered.

The school's financial status wavered over the next year, dipping and rising intermittently. At the April 1950 board meeting, McKinney again presented his resignation. By then the board was so eager to rid Storer of McKinney that they not only accepted his resignation but also made it effective a month earlier (July 1) than he had originally suggested. A month later, a board of three faculty members was elected to supervise the daily administration of Storer College until a new president could be hired. McKinney left the campus in May after the close of commencement activities to assume an administrative appointment at Morgan State College in Baltimore. With McKinney's departure, the tenure of the black college's first black president came to a resounding close.

AFTER MCKINNEY: STORER'S FINAL DAYS

For two years after McKinney's resignation in 1950 an Interim Administrative Committee appointed by the Board of Trustees managed Storer College. The commission, chaired by Leroy Dennis Johnson, a faculty member and dean of men, remained in operation until May 1952, when Rev. Leonard Earl Terrell was selected to manage the various branches of the school's interests. Terrell was the last principal administrator in the history of the school.

The 1952 Homecoming Court

For the two years before Terrell was named president, however, the three-member Administrative Committee was in charge of Storer College. This meant handling not just the day-to-day responsibilities but also dealing with the unenviable task of making crucial decisions about keeping the college open. To keep the college afloat financially, the decision was made to sell "surplus lots" and apply monies earned from these sales back into the coffers. Despite ongoing financial woes, efforts were made to recruit additional students.

By 1951, a search committee had identified four potential replacements for McKinney, with the front-runner being Dr. Herbert Miller, presently at the Baptist Educational Center in New York City, who was invited to interview in June. However, on the day of Miller's scheduled visit, the Executive Committee reported that it had been cancelled, somewhat mysteriously, "in the best interest of the College." The Executive Committee then voted to disband the Administrative Committee and hire Dean Leroy Johnson in dual roles as vice-president and Dean of the college simultaneously. This dual roles had been a long-standing, accepted tradition; however, it had evolved to become one of the college's most dysfunctional aspects. Consequently, in a few months, Johnson requested that the Administrative Committee be reformed because the responsibilities, duties, and obligations were beyond the capabilities of one person.

A brief student interlude

At this time, the financial outlook for the school was at least marginally improved. The deficit was gone, the potential for a balanced budget positive, and additional buildings—including Lockwood House—were being sold to raise more money. Unfortunately, the air of optimism was short-lived. Enrollment soon declined and the college was forced to borrow money. In 1952, the school's vice-president recommended that a committee be formed to look into selling off school property. The school's second candidate for president, Dr. Charles Boddie, minister of Mt. Olivet Baptist Church in Rochester, New York, declined to accept the position, presumably not liking the direction of the school's momentum.

At the Board of Trustees' 1952 meeting, the news was announced that the college finally had a president, Reverend L. E. Terrell. Terrell's short tenure seemed destined to fail, given the larger issues then at hand. The school entered its 1952–53 academic year with a deficit that amounted to $11,855.

Despite Terrell's enthusiasm and the welcome addition of a library annex to the campus, by February 1953, the Board of Trustees was already in serious deliberations over the future of Storer. The school's situation as a Christian college meant that it had long relied on support from the Free Will and regular Baptist denominations. This dependency placed its future in financial peril, with little hope of assistance from outside sources. The board appealed to the American Baptist Convention for financial aid, but "little hope" was offered. The Convention's representative did suggest that the school begin a "Build Storer" campaign that focused on increasing enrollment, raising more funds from alumni, and receiving additional assistance from churches.

Several factors impeded Storer from making progress on these goals, including its lack of regional accreditation. This left potential supporters in a dilemma. Storer's library and gymnasium were outdated, and its tuition was higher than those of state schools. By late 1953, there were only fifty boarding students and twenty-one day students. A last-ditch effort was made to raise money by mortgaging Brackett House.

Although at the end of 1953, a special board was convened to study the college's potential, Storer College's days were numbered. While some additional funds were received, they were not enough, and the Executive Committee "finally faced the hard reality that Storer College could not continue in its current condition." Its members recommended to the Board of Trustees that the college suspend operations for 1954–55. At the board's next meeting, members of the Alumni Association convinced them to keep the school open, promising that they would contribute additional funding.

The Alumni Association's "Save Storer" campaign began and met with some initial success. It raised $5,000 for scholarships and recruited more students than Storer had had for several years. Financially, however, the school still wavered. The next meeting of the Board of Trustees proved monumental for several reasons. First, although President Terrell had always managed to maintain hope—in October 1954, in fact, he had attempted to "rally" the Board regarding the school's future—at the April 1955 Board meeting, he tendered his resignation. Second and more portentous was news the board received from the state. The groundbreaking *Brown v. Board of Education of Topeka, Kansas* had been decided, effectively ending educational segregation. The State of West Virginia determined that it would no longer support Storer financially, since Storer's students were then eligible for acceptance under the public school boards. The state believed that it could no longer justify either its appropriations to Storer College nor any longer continue to finance a dual system of education. With a total debt level of $35,000, Storer College could not go on. The board's decision was to terminate the operation of the school with the outgoing class of 1955.

After nearly ninety years of existence, after surviving local resistance, two world wars, and the Great Depression, Storer College graduated its class of 1955 and closed its doors as an educational institution. It is more than symbolic that its final years were marked by the sale or mortgaging of two of its original buildings—the Lockwood and Brackett houses. Although the Board of Trustees met on a regular basis and even attempted to resurrect the school, it was not to be. This did not mean, however, that the school would fade into memory. In 1963, the National Park Service took control of the "campus and grounds" under the protective aegis of the Harpers Ferry National Park.

LEGAL CHALLENGES AND
THE FEDERAL ACQUISITION, 1955

Storer's Future: Two Decisions, Two Proposals, Two Directions

After the landmark 1954 *Brown v. Board of Education of Topeka, Kansas* decision, the federal court system mandated that the attorney general of each state must implement the decision to desegregate public schools. West Virginia was no exception. When Chief Justice Warren read the decision into the nation's public record, school districts began to implement the decision of the high court "with all deliberate speed" desegregating the nation's schools. Thereafter, the West Virginia's State Legislature, in compliance with the federal mandate, voted to discontinue its annual $20,000 appropriation to Storer College. Without much debate, Storer's Board of Trustees realized that the school could not make up such a deficit. In a last-ditch effort to keep the school afloat financially, the board and its convention proceeded to circulate requests for proposals designed to solicit aid. Two proposals—the Alderson-Broaddus Proposal and the Zion Proposal— came quickly.

ALDERSON-BROADDUS PROPOSAL

The first proposal—under the auspices of the Alderson-Broaddus College in Philippi, West Virginia—arrived for consideration on

September 11, 1958. The Executive Committee of Alderson-Broaddus understood that the "purposes and ideals of Storer

Alderson-Broaddus

College" were to be effected through "some other" institution in order to avoid the additional expense of maintaining a "separate educational institution" specifically for minority students. It recommended that negotiations begin with a collaborative board for the express purpose of determining the possibility of the institutional mergers. The Alderson-Broaddus Executive Committee submitted a four-point recommendation. First, the committee agreed that the name of Storer College should be preserved "in some significant way" on the Phillipi campus. Second, the committee agreed to accept the transfer of alumni records. Third, the members agreed to accept representation on the school's general "College Board." Finally, they would accept the "transfer of resources," reserving a portion for endowing scholarships designed to support the school's emphasis on Negro education. Slightly more than a month after the Alderson-Broaddus Proposal was received, a second arrived for board members to consider.

THE ZION PROPOSAL

On October 28, the Zion Proposal reached Storer College's Board of Trustees. By arrangement of its "National Officers and the Bishops," the African Methodist Episcopal Zion Church (AMEZC) convened an "all-day conference" in order to form a "tentative proposal" for consideration by the Storer College Board of Trustees. Like the Free Will Baptists during the nineteenth century, the "Zionites" had extended their influence through missionaries.

The AMEZC formed an "ad hoc Negotiations Committee" to act as liaison between the school board and the church polity. The committee then proceeded to develop an eight-point proposal. First, the original name of the institution would be retained. Second, its physical plant would be used and maintained in its present location. Third, the AMEZC acknowledged that it would assume total responsibility for managing the reopening, operation, maintenance, and perpetuation of the school. Fourth, a physical building renovation schedule was included assuring that the AMEZC would refurbish campus buildings. Fifth, programs were designed at a reasonable pace in order to correspond with the renovation plan. Sixth, the denomination proposed relocating several of its current operations to Harpers Ferry. Seventh, a new Board of Trustees was conceived, with the board's composition was proposed as 30 percent Free Will Baptist and 60 percent AMEZC. Finally, if the proposal was "acceptable to all parties," the details were to be "negotiated" with all "formalities" to transpire and action "undertaken immediately" to quickly bring Storer College back to a state of educational readiness. The board now had to choose between two roughly equivalent proposals for maintaining Storer College.

ACCOUNTABILITY: TWO ALUMNI BRING SUIT

The majority of the Board of Trustees voted to accept the Alderson-Broaddus Proposal and liquidate Storer's assets, but Mary Peyton Dyson and Madison Spenser Briscoe did not. They were decidedly against the liquidation of the school's assets and against abandoning the physical plant, feeling certain that Storer College's memory was in jeopardy of extinction. Dyson and Briscoe firmly believed the board should reconsider its opinion. They spoke of potential liabilities associated with "donors of endowments and contributors" who had invested in the school, violations to the school's original 1867 legislative charter, and breaches to the existing "Act to Incorporate" between the institution and the state government.

A CASE FOR LITIGATION

Barely three months later, on February 11, 1959, Carlisle E. Pratt filed a civil suit on behalf of Dyson and Briscoe in the United States District County for the District of Columbia. Pratt's "Motion for Preliminary Injunction" was meant to prevent a "Special Committee" appointed by Clarence Cranford, heading the board during the closing decade, from beginning the process of liquidating Storer's assets. By filing suit,

Transitions and Endings

Dyson and Briscoe hoped to prevent any further action by the committee until specific questions involving the college's historical integrity, liquid and fixed assets, and real properties could be fully explored. Their subsequent litigation sets forth the belief that the proposal from the AMEZC "lends hope and restoration . . . in the future operation of said Storer College," which of course was their chief goal.

After Washington's District Court remanded the case back to West Virginia, it was a foregone conclusion that the school would be closed. Storer College's future was sealed.

THE MERGER

In 1960, the Storer College Board of Trustees appointed a "Special Committee." Cranford worked through this committee to design a plan for keeping the major interests and concerns that had led to the founding of the college funded. The committee's final proposal recommended "the sale of the property, the liquidation of all indebtedness [and decreed that] the remaining assets of Storer College [were to] be given in equal portions to Virginia Union University, Richmond, Virginia and to Alderson-Broaddus College, Philippi, West Virginia . . . [since] all three parties to this contact are Baptist schools which are sponsored by the American Baptist Convention." So, in 1960, Storer College officially merged with Virginia Union University.

All of the liquid assets such as investments, endowments, and interest-bearing accounts were transferred to Alderson-Broaddus. The state's primary educational facility, West Virginia University, received the school's administrative records, including correspondences and financial documents. Although the merger and liquidation of assets closed Storer College, the institutional memory of the school was then and still remains to be promoted by a dedicated alumni association.

"WHEREAS, Storer College, Inc. (formerly The President and Trustees of Storer College), a West Virginia non-stock corporation . . . has been closed as a school for higher education, and Virginia Union University is able to render a service to the territory formerly served by Storer College similar to that formerly rendered by Storer College; and WHEREAS, it appears that a merger of Storer College, Inc. into Virginia Union University, upon the terms and conditions hereinafter set forth, will enable Virginia Union University to perpetuate the aims, ideals and purpose for which Storer College was founded, and would serve the best interests of both institutions . . . have agreed upon all provisions, terms and conditions of such merger . . . shall be effected upon the following terms, provisions, conditions, stipulations, and agreements."

Terms of the 1960 merger between Storer College and Virginia Union University

Legacy

An up-river view of the ferry town's confluence

THE RETURN TO FEDERAL MANAGEMENT

The facilities that housed Storer College once belonged to the federal government, so it was perhaps fitting that once the school closed, the campus reverted to its former owners. The return of the Storer College campus to federal management, and the decision that led to its inclusion in the "national monument" at Harpers Ferry after 1955, is tied to Storer's Dr. Henry McDonald, president of Storer College from 1899 to 1944. He played a vital role in the formation and establishment of the Harper's Ferry National Monument erected in Harpers Ferry to commemorate John Brown's insurrection on the United States Federal Arsenal on October 17, 1859.

THE HARPERS FERRY NATIONAL MONUMENT

In 1936, Harpers Ferry sustained a horrific flood that precipitated an abrupt spring thaw in the West Virginia upper highlands and along the Virginia and Maryland borders. Such destructive, natural convergence was not unknown in the natural scheme of West Virginia's winter-to-spring transition, but this flood proved far more devastating.

After the thirty-six-foot water wall gushed through the town's rivers, local officials and state representatives were confronted with an extensive damage report. Among the town's officials was Storer's President McDonald, an active member of the community since his first arrival in 1899. Representing the state's assessment team was Jennings Randolph, then West Virginia's United States congressman for its Second Congressional District. Both men

Stone piers of the former B&O Railroad's Bollman Bridge washed out in the 1936 flood

simultaneously agreed that an appeal should be made to the Department of the Interior under the United States Congress in order to preserve the important local historical buildings and battlefields.

Aerial view of the "Point" at Harpers Ferry, looking east, showing (left to right) the new B&O Bridge, completed in 1931

Over the next several years, the two men collaborated on an integrated design that would save the town's historical sites. Finally, they agreed on plans involving the construction of a national highway. One highway was to follow the Potomac River from Washington into Harpers Ferry with a northerly spur into Pennsylvania. Another plan involved a highway extending southward from Harpers Ferry to Front Royal, Virginia. If combined, the two proposed designs—from Front Royal northwestward to Sharpsburg, Maryland, and, at its furthermost northern point, to Gettysburg, Pennsylvania—would have been significant. Although the fundamental objective of the project is not clearly stated, when one takes into consideration McDonald's affection and Randolph's enthusiasm for Civil War history, at least one deduction is apparent. The proposed highway would have encompassed the military routes of numerous Civil War generals from both sides.

To launch the project, local and state representatives approached representatives at the federal level. In 1937, Randolph's office contacted representatives of the National Park Service. They, in turn, "conducted an extensive inquiry and survey" of the area that included the triangulated apex of three states' mountainous heights in Maryland (Maryland Heights), Virginia (Loudoun Heights), and West Virginia (Bolivar Heights) in order to determine the "desirability [for] inclusion" under federal jurisdiction directed by the National Park Consortium.

The following year, in 1938, the project stepped closer to certainty when McDonald and Randolph spearheaded a public forum to discuss the ferry town's inclusion under federal jurisdiction. McDonald and Randolph invited the general public, historians, administrators, and elected officials from the three states whose state boundaries and real properties were named in the proposal. According to Chief Historian Dennis Frye, "over 200 participants" converged in the area to offer input. The focus of this formative meeting, held on February 17, was twofold. First, to involve the public voice and secondly, to investigate how each state would assume its share of financial responsibilities and divide real properties in conjunction with a collaborative plan that included the federal government.

While Randolph solicited political support in Washington for the park, McDonald prepared to retire from his administrative position at Storer College. After McDonald participated in Storer's "Commencement Exercises" the first weekend in June 1944, he was notified three weeks later, on June 30, 1944, that the historic "monument" was imminent. This perhaps reinvigorated the emeritus president with a sense of renewed hope and usefulness. When President Franklin Delano Roosevelt signed a bill to institute a "national monument" at Harpers Ferry, West Virginia, the bill's stipulations provided only for an official "authorization" for the National Park Service "to accept 1,500 acres of donated" state properties in the immediate vicinity. No real federal appropriations were yet allotted to the general project.

By 1948, it became evident in the surrounding region that the town's potential as a park remained in jeopardy. Several buildings were in dire need of repair, general cleanup, and debris removal. Eventually state agencies, historical societies, and area residents collaborated long enough to keep the project viable until the state's elected officials took a vested interest in the project's resurrection.

On March 12, 1951, three West Virginia elected officials reinvigorated the project. Harley O. Staggers, a congressman, garnered support in favor of the park, working as liaison between state and federal appropriators to obtain funding. Okey L. Patteson, the state's governor, prompted

the legislature to allocate $350,000 to purchase another 514 acres to add to the park. Finally, Gilbert Perry, the mayor of Harpers Ferry, proceeded with "title searches and property acquisition."

On January 16, 1953, Governor Patteson transferred a deed for four hundred acres to the Department of the Interior to be used expressly for the establishment of the Harpers Ferry National Monument. One year later, in 1954, John T. Willett was commissioned as the park's first superintendent.

McDonald did not live long enough to see these efforts come to fruition. After McDonald retired in 1944, he worked with the incoming administrator, President Richard McKinney, for a period in order to help McKinney acclimate to the campus, town, and student affairs. Having lived a life of continuous activity, however, McDonald never fully retired from activities connected with the school, town, or the many state organizations to which he belonged. He died in November 1951, four years before Storer College graduated its last class, and a full nine years before the campus reverted, in 1960, to the ownership of the federal government.

THE NATIONAL PARK SERVICE

On July 14, 1960, Public Law 86-655 placed the campus of Storer College again in the control of federal hands. The process by which this occurred had been several months in the making. On March 1 of that year, in the House of Representatives, Jennings B. Randolph sponsored legislation providing for the federal takeover of the campus, a bill taken to the floor by Harley O. Staggers. The legislation proposed by Randolph called to "authorize the acquisition of certain lands including the Storer College site, John Brown's Fort site, and the Federal armory, for addition to Harper's Ferry National Monument." In the United States Senate, the bill was sponsored by West Virginia Senator Robert C. Byrd and was passed in amended form on April 11. On July 2, it was passed to the House Committee on Interior and Insular Affairs. Finally, it became law.

When the National Parks Service took control of Storer College, it acquired thirty acres of fixed structures and real properties to add to its national inventory of protected and preserved sites. Part of this process involved rehabilitating those structures the agency felt it could save, while demolishing others. In 1962, for example, improvements were made to several campus buildings and others were relocated to restore historical

On September 21, 1967, Congressman Harley O. Staggers (WV) in company with Senator Jennings Randolph (WV), William C. Everhart (manager, Harpers Ferry Center), Stewart Udall, U.S. secretary of the interior; and Senator Robert C. Byrd (WV), arrange for an official photograph during the architectural model unveiling for the Harpers Ferry Interpretive Design Center (HF-IDC) scheduled for construction the following year in April. These three elected West Virginia representatives were instrumental in preserving the Storer College campus under the protective aegis of the United States Department of the Interior.

integrity. Cook Hall, instituted originally as a dormitory for male students, was improved by the Department of the Interior for "use by visiting National Park Service personnel." Other buildings were, however, demolished by the National Park Service that same year, including Mosher (originally Myrtle) Hall, Brackett Hall (formerly Lincoln Hall, the former men's dormitory), Jackson and Sinclair cottages, and the Kent and Saunders houses. The DeWolf Industrial Building and the Storer College Gymnasium were likewise razed. Later, the Science Building, originally built in the 1940s, was also demolished.

Despite the destruction, some of the campus's most historic buildings were given new leases on life. During the 1960s Lockwood House, which in 1865 had housed both the Shenandoah Mission and the Harpers Ferry Mission School, benefited from a partial restoration project. Two main-floor rooms were "restored and the basement [was subsequently] used for artifact storage." Likewise, Morrell House, used during Storer's operation by the Alexander Hatch Morrell family, was refurbished and maintained in its original location to house the executive-level administrator. The park's superintendent operates from this location on Camp Hill today.

The Mather Training Center was the first such federal training center established in West Virginia's Eastern Panhandle. Its progressive advancement includes "courses, workshops, and distance learning opportunities" for municipal and federal representatives. Today, the Mather Training Center facility also encompasses Wirth Hall, named for Conrad Wirth, which provides access to "classrooms and administrative offices," and Cook Hall Dormitory, which is used as additional office space for park service staff. In 1970, the federal agency opened its Interpretative Design Center, which is adjacent to the Mather Training Center in Anthony Hall. The purpose of the design center is to organize, coordinate, and produce maps, exhibits, and film projects. In an effort to meet instructional demands, the Mather Center coordinates training and development programs for administrators, managers, supervisors, coordinators, and specialists, including a "fast rack, two-year intake trainee program."

Additionally, the Curtis Free Will Baptist Church, also known as the Curtis Memorial Baptist Chapel, named in honor of Silas Curtis in 1893, remains a vital structure for the park service. The main auditorium in the building continues to be utilized as a meeting, conference,

and congregational structure by municipal, organizational, and federal assemblies. The SCNAA culminates its annual reunion event each year by holding its closing exercises in the Curtis Free Will Baptist Church.

Since 1960, then, the National Park Service has put its own stamp on the campus that once served as the home of Storer College, razing several key structures while maintaining others. Yet, its continued use of the campus as more than simply a national park—as also a training center and as a campus open to public gatherings, including meetings of the SCNAA—indicates the agency's willingness to further the original mission of the school and its Free Will Baptist "founders and fathers."

The Continuing Use of Storer College Campus

Although Storer College concluded its almost one-hundred-year-role as a Negro college in 1955, through its new life as a national park site, the Storer College campus continues to impact the public mind and maintain its place in regional and national history. It has been the site of numerous dramatizations, seminars, and programs designed to highlight the history of the college and its town, gives insight into the Civil War and Reconstruction periods, and conveys the stories of the many individuals associated with its genesis, development, contributions, demise, and legacy.

Photo Credits

About the Author

Dawne Raines Burke, Ph.D., is an assistant professor of Education to the Department of Education, School of Education & Professional Studies at Shepherd University, located in historic Shepherdstown, West Virginia. Burke is an instructor in the Teacher Education Program where she provides instruction across the curriculum in sociology, psychology, research methodology, and diversity issues to over seven hundred prospective teaching candidates. Burke received her undergraduate degrees from Shepherd, later attending West Virginia University and receiving a master's degree in secondary education from the College of Human Resources & Education. Her doctoral degree in human development was conferred upon her in 2004 by Virginia Polytechnic Institute & State University. Her dissertation entitled, "Storer College: A Hope for Redemption in the Shadow of Slavery, 1865–1955," was a national finalist for the Beeman Award. Bestowed by the Council for Advancement and Support of Education (CASE), the Beeman Award "recognize[s] excellence in writing about educational advancement" in America at the doctoral level. Burke was also recognized in 2005 by the Storer College National Alumni Association for her many contributions to preserve Storer's institutional narrative.

Burke has written several articles on the subject of Storer College, including an article trilogy based on the life of Dr. Nnamdi "Zik" Azikiwe, the High Owelle of Onitsha and the first elected president of the Republic of Nigeria, who graduated from Storer College in 1927.

The author is currently participating in two film projects. The first is an independent, grant-funded, federal partnership documentary film based on Storer College, produced and directed by Midge Flinn Yost. The second is a feature film to be aired on *Outlook* for West Virginia Public Broadcasting Service, produced by Bob Wilkinson.

Burke is also the mother of two incredibly gifted children—Logan Gray and D. Michael Burke, III.

The Fiftieth Anniversary of the
Closing of *Storer College*